# GOD
## SIGHTINGS

# GOD
## SIGHTINGS

in Healthcare Missions Around the World

Compiled by
## TRISH BURGESS, MD

**Christian
Medical & Dental
Associations®**
*Changing Hearts in Healthcare*

The Christian Medical & Dental Associations was founded in 1931 and currently serves more than 18,000 members. It coordinates a network of Christian healthcare professionals for personal and professional growth; sponsors student ministries in medical and dental schools; conducts overseas healthcare projects for underserved populations; addresses policies on healthcare, medical ethics and bioethical and human rights issues; distributes educational and inspirational resources; provides missionary healthcare professionals with continuing education resources; and conducts international academic exchange programs.

For more information:
Christian Medical & Dental Associations
P.O. Box 7500
Bristol, TN 37621-7500
888-230-2637
*www.cmda.org • main@cmda.org*

Editing by Mandi Morrin
Cover design and interior layout by Terry Bailey

ISBN: 978-1-7344968-3-3
Library of Congress Control Number: 2022930505

Printed in the United States of America
First Printing March 2022

To all our GHO staff and team leaders.
Your dedication and commitment to bringing the gospel
to the nations and ministering through healthcare
has blessed thousands around the world.

With a grateful heart to our Lord and Savior
Jesus Christ, who invites us to join Him and participate
in His work to the ends of the earth.

# FOREWORD

If you have had the privilege of participating in healthcare missions internationally, either short-term or long-term, then you will likely understand the premise of a "God sighting." Dr. Trish Burgess has served as Director of Global Health Outreach since 2018, and she decided to turn an incredibly challenging season of ministry with COVID-19 travel restrictions into an opportunity to write about God's amazing deeds, as experienced over the years by GHO team participants and their team leaders. Dr. Burgess has compiled for us a treasure trove of stories that demonstrate how God cares for and intervenes in the lives of the most poor and needy and lost souls on the planet through His willing servants in healthcare.

Our lives in service through healthcare, as God's sons and daughters, are full of privilege but with a degree of paradox. I suggest "paradox," because Paul told us, "For we live by faith not by sight" (2 Corinthians 5:7, NIV), and he also told us, "So we fix our eyes not on what is seen, but on what is unseen, since what is seen is temporary, but what is unseen is eternal" (2 Corinthians 4:18, NIV).

"God sightings" are only possible because the Spirit of God helps us to "see" what God is doing in or through or around us during times of cross-cultural service in healthcare that only He could have orchestrated. Solomon tells us that if we have eyes to see, it is because God gave us the gift of vision (Proverbs 20:12). I believe these stories will inspire you and remind you that our God is an ever-present help in times of sickness, trouble and danger.

Mike Chupp, MD, FACS
CEO, Christian Medical & Dental Associations

# TABLE OF CONTENTS

# INTRODUCTION

"And He sent them out to proclaim the kingdom of God and to perform healing" (Luke 9:2, NASB).

Every time I travel on the mission field, I pray to be the hands and feet of Jesus to those we are serving. On the mission field I see Jesus in the very people we are there to help. And every mission is an encounter with our living God. Mission teams are comprised of all kinds of people, from physicians, dentists, nurses and pharmacists to all allied health specialties and even non-medical servants.

On GHO mission trips we have morning and evening praise and worship, devotions and testimonies. At the end of every day, team members report "God sightings," remarkable firsthand accounts of where, when and how they witnessed Almighty God at work. This book is full of God sightings by ordinary, and yet extraordinary, people who put their trust in God. People who left the comforts of home and family, culture and even language to fully rely on God to walk with them and work in and through them as they take the gospel to the nations. Ordinary people who had the courage to say yes.

If you have been camping out in your comfort zone for far too long, I'm prayerful this book will encourage you to say yes to international missions and give God a chance to show Himself to you. And then come join us on a GHO mission trip! You will love it.

Trish Burgess, MD
Director, Global Health Outreach

# AFGHANISTAN
## 33.9391° N, 67.7100° E

## I Am a Follower of Jesus
*Sam Molind, DMD*

It was in early March 2004 that GHO had the opportunity to partner with SOZO and Cure International Hospital to serve in Afghanistan. The decades of civil turmoil and war had obviously left its devastating mark on the most vulnerable, Afghan women and children. One of every 12 mothers died from the complications of childbirth. One in every four children died before they celebrated their fifth birthday, and the life expectancy was 42 years—35 of which may be "healthy" years.

For years, Afghanistan had been under oppressive control, first the warlords, then the Soviet Communist regime and finally the vicious Taliban. The Taliban regime, a radical Islamic movement, took control of Kabul, Afghanistan in September 1996. Women were under great persecution and were prisoners within their own country. Before the Taliban took control of the country, women made up 70 percent of the teaching force, and 40 percent of the city's physicians were women. Afghan women who were once free to choose what they wore and pursue careers became subject to harsh punishments. Under the Taliban, women had less access to hospitals. The Taliban also banned female hospital personnel from working. In fact, there were no women in medical schools or practicing medicine under Taliban rule. Due to their religious beliefs, men could not examine women who were not wearing full clothing. This made it very difficult for women to have female exams or be examined properly during pregnancy. This was one of the reasons for the high infant mortality rates and some of the highest death rates for mothers dying in childbirth in the world! It was at that time so important for us to have female physicians on our teams. In fact, if we did not have female physicians, women would not be allowed to come to our clinics, and in turn they could not bring their children for care. It was into this war-torn area the Lord had called us and opened a door to give witness to the love and the compassion of our precious Lord Jesus.

We were on the road to Istalef, an internally displaced persons town, when I remembered passing a rusting hulk of a Russian tank, its gun pointing to the sky in a last attempt to appeal to a higher power to help as it died on that dusty, hard, desolate hillside. I wondered how many men died in that one place. The smell of death swirled around me like little dust demons. It just seemed so hard, so dry, so barren and so unforgiving. How had we come to this, we who pride ourselves on honor, gentleness, hospitality and brotherly love? How did men who never met, had never spoken, hate each other so vehemently? The time passed quickly and we reached Istalef. No crowds were waiting. We set up our clinics and still no one arrived. This was an unusual situation, particularly knowing the intense needs for medical and dental care. I asked Wakeel, the interpreter, "Why do you think no one has shown up?" He replied, "I believe the regional Imam has spoken to the people and forbid them to come to our clinics." I asked, "Can we find him and speak to him?" Wakeel gave me a strange look but agreed to look for him with me.

The Imam found us while we were looking for him and asked, "Were you looking for me?" I don't believe I have ever seen such piercing eyes as his. "Are you an American?" he asked. I answered, "Yes." He then questioned, "Are you a Christian?" I replied, "I am a follower of Jesus." He went on to say, "You are a Christian, and an American, and 50 percent of your marriages end in divorce, you have killed more than 50,000 unborn children, all the 'X rated' films and pornography we have has come from your country and if that is what liberty brings and Christianity has to offer, I do not want my people to have any of it!"

I was shocked and ashamed, but I pulled myself together and said, "I am very ashamed of all you have mentioned about my country, and I can assure you that all of my team members are followers of Jesus and despise the things you mentioned. We all have come here to demonstrate our love and the love and compassion of Jesus to you. All we ask is for the opportunity to serve you, please give us an opportunity to prove ourselves!" His response was, "We will see about that!" and he walked away.

When I arrived back at the clinic, we went to prayer and were made acutely aware the glasses we look through and the impressions we have about ourselves were not the same image he had of us. The Lord had given us an open door and a very important, humbling lesson. That afternoon the displaced people of Istalef came in droves to the clinic and met humble bond servants of the risen Lord, praising Him and looking forward to serving the least, the lost and the last. Along with the people came the Imam. He and I had the opportunity to talk again, and every year thereafter he would find me and we would have wonderful conversations. In the end, I think he may have become a seeker. Praise Jesus!

# CAMBODIA
## 12.5657° N, 104.9910° E

## Understanding the Gospel
*Mike O'Callaghan, DDS*

In February 2012, we were in Cambodia for our third annual GHO mission trip to this Southeast Asian nation. When our two rented buses pulled up to a large old wooden building after a 90-minute ride on dusty roads, we saw about 200 patients already waiting to be treated. It was our fourth clinic day, so the team had already learned the ropes and were able to hit the ground running.

About 11 a.m., Scott, a member of our optical team, noticed that a young boy's eyes looked unusual to him. It also appeared he was clinically blind by the way his mother was leading him around. Scott came over to me in the dental area to discuss this. Together we brought the mother and her son to our pediatrician, Marty. A history and exam were followed by some phone calls to national partners who were not with us. One such call was to Phnom Penh, to a godly Cambodian ophthalmologist I had met on our first mission trip to Cambodia. It was determined that this 8-year-old boy might suffer from bilateral congenital cataracts. We identified a different ophthalmologist much closer, in Siem Reap, where our hotel was. The estimated cost to treat both eyes was about $400, which we had raised beforehand for such incidents.

Another national partner, also a physician, adamantly told me, "You must get this boy to the doctor today! Tomorrow never happens in Cambodia." But when I discussed this with the boy's mother, she refused to leave with her son and nursing baby to travel to Siem Reap for the needed care. I was fortunate to have the translation assistance of Khema, a Cambodian medical student who was a Christian, having been saved helping on a mission trip three years earlier.

Khema talked with the boy's mother and learned she had five children. Her husband often got drunk and was physically abusive. If she were not there to protect the children, they might be injured by their father. Thus, the mother asked if she could arrange to bring her other children to a relative's home and return tomorrow morning with the boy and her nursing baby for the trip to Siem Reap.

By God's grace, this location was the only one we would return to during our eight clinic days. So, we agreed to do that. This entire process took about two hours. Toward the end of our time together, Khema enthusiastically told me, "The mother wants to hear about Jesus." Khema used her Evangecube and shared the good news with the mother. A few minutes later as she finished, Khema said, "The mother wants to become Christian." Khema then led the mother in a prayer of salvation. A moment later, Khema said with delight, "The boy wants to become Christian too." She then led the boy in a repeat-after-me salvation prayer.

While I was happy to see this transpire, my heart and mind were somewhat conflicted. This was because I had been wrestling with understanding what truly constitutes the gospel and how to best share it in such cross-cultural environments on short-term healthcare mission trips without resulting in large numbers of false professions of faith. At that time, I was leading three GHO trips each year where about 7,000 people heard the gospel. Some of these patients, like this mother and her son, lived in unreached areas with little to no exposure to Christianity. I made a mental note to talk with Khema the following day, on the bus ride back to our hotel.

In answer to much prayer, when we arrived at the same clinic site the next day, the mother was standing there with a baby in arms and her 8-year-old son at her side. A private car had been hired to follow us out of town. After a prayer for God's divine assistance, we sent them off to the hospital.

Later that afternoon, I went over to Khema and asked if she would save a spot for me next to her on the bus ride back to hotel. I wanted to catch up with her, as she had served with us on the previous two GHO mission trips. She agreed. As we were traveling back to the hotel for a much-needed weekend break, I enjoyed conversing with Khema. I learned more about her family, her schooling and the godly young man she hoped to marry after graduation.

Toward the end of our travel time, I asked her as nonchalantly as I could: "Khema, I would like to ask you some questions about the mother and her blind son to help me better gain a better understanding. Would that be okay?"

Khema looked surprised yet agreed. I asked what she thought the mother's religious worldview was yesterday as she walked into our clinic. Basically, it was as I expected, what has been described as "folk Buddhism," a mixture of Buddhist religious tradition comingled with deeply animistic roots. The concept of one true God, of eternal life, of substitutionary atonement and of grace would be entirely foreign concepts. I then asked Khema what she thought the mother understood after hearing the gospel presentation. Khema immediately looked offended, which I was carefully trying to avoid. "Dr. Mike," she said, "You think I did a bad job sharing the gospel?"

I assured Khema that I held her in the highest regard (which was a fact), but I was seeking more understanding so I might better fulfill my responsibilities as a GHO team leader.

Khema's facial expression continued to reveal hurt feelings. I continued, explaining how I was in the midst of reading several theology books about what comprises the gospel on cross-cultural ministry. So, I asked my question again saying, "Khema, I don't speak any Khmer. And I doubt I ever will. I greatly value your perspective. I seek your input to help me. So please tell me, what do you think the mother understood after hearing the gospel yesterday?"

Khema took a breath and said, "Dr. Mike, I think she thought the same thing that I thought when I heard the gospel about three years ago from a classmate. I knew it was true, the true story from the one true God. I was raised in a Buddhist family. No one in my family was Christian. But I heard the gospel just like I told the mother yesterday. I believed the gospel and I became Christian. Is something wrong with that?" My heart melted. "No, Khema," I said with tears flowing down my face. "Nothing is wrong with that at all. It is really beautiful. Thank you so much. I have learned more from you than I might learn from reading several big theology books."

Over the next month or so, the young boy had both eyes treated. Marty, our GHO pediatrician, was able to visit them at the hospital after his first eye was successfully treated before flying home.

Khema married that young man after graduating from medical school. Both are now serving the Lord in full-time vocational ministry in rural Cambodia.

I am still trying to better understand and apply the glorious gospel in my own life and ministry.

## The Lord's Mountain
### *Dorothy Molind, Non-medical Servant*

One afternoon Trudy, our partnering missionary, asked if I wanted to go further up the mountain and see if we could find a family. She had ministered to them a few years ago when she was traveling these mountains. Never to be one to shrink from a new adventure, two other teammates and I hopped into the back of a rickety old truck she was driving.

About 20 minutes later we left the main road and began a slow laborious climb over terrain never meant to be traversed by motorized vehicles. By this time none of us in the back were sure she knew where she was going, yet onward the old truck toiled, Trudy carefully picking the route of least resistance. Eventually, as promised, we drove past one remote house, then another needing just as much repair as the first, until we came to an abrupt halt in front of what appeared to be three connected homes.

Trudy, from Germany, had been a missionary to China for the last 15 years. Her command of Mandarin is commendable, and she immediately engaged the first person we saw in conversation. Within moments she was surrounded by 10 to 12 excited Chinese peasants. Everyone seemed to recognize her, and as their excitement grew, so did the crowd.

While everyone's attention was focused on Trudy, it gave the three of us time to survey this tiny little hamlet. The "houses" were all two stories high and hungry for repair. The ground floor housed all the animals and a small area for their hotpot. Above the animals, and their stench, on the second level was what appeared to be the family area.

A few moments into our observations, Trudy waved us over to where she stood talking with an elderly gentleman and it was picture time! It was evident the man was insistent on standing in one particular spot from which his picture was to be taken. We willingly obliged. Soon formalities were over, the goodbyes said and we were back in the vehicle rolling down the mountainside just ahead of the encroaching darkness.

Relieved to be back on the main road Trudy pulled over and recounted how two years ago when she first visited the village the young son of the gentleman was gravely ill. The family had no money nor transportation to take him down the mountain to Dong Wong for medical treatment. Trudy, ever generous, had given the family money to cover the expenses. Not only had the boy survived, he thrived! Today, much to Trudy's surprise, the man related how he had been saving for the last two years from his paltry earnings of selling his goats confident that one day "the woman who carried a Bible" would return and he could repay her.

But what about all the fuss when we were taking his picture, we asked? He was so insistent where he stood as we took his picture. Trudy replied, "He wanted to be sure the distant mountain was in the background." He said, "That was where the Lord lived." He called it The Lord's Mountain. "...'On the mount of the Lord it shall be provided'" (Genesis 22:14b, ESV). Indeed, for him and his family in the shadow of the Mountain of the Lord it had been provided.

## The Blind Will See
*Nate Bernard, MDiv*

I was co-leading a mission team in the Dominican Republic and had the opportunity to witness a miracle at our clinic in the optometry area. After talking more to our vision team, this story became even more incredible. First, it was the first time we have ever had an optometrist on our team. Second, it was the first time and may be the last time we see this batey (sugarcane work village), as we see three new ones each trip and there are numerous bateys.

Before our team leaves on a mission trip, we plan and pack all of our medications and supplies. The prescription glasses our eye doctor had at his disposal had been donated and the strength of each lens recorded. Obviously, he could not make custom prescription glasses in the Dominican Republic. For the most part, the right eye and left eye are pretty close in visual acuity.

A young girl named Ana came to our clinic. She had an obvious eye problem and vision deficit from birth. When you looked at her, her right eye was deviated so severely that you could almost see nothing but the white part of her eye. It was severely turned toward the left eye. Her left eye looked straight forward. This made it extremely difficult for her to see correctly, if at all.

The optometrist evaluated Ana. It turned out she had a rare vision discrepancy between her two eyes. The correction of her vision requirements between her eyes was dramatic. Her right eye required a much stronger lens than her left eye. Each lens has three different measurements to accurately fit the need of each eye. Our doctor had an exact fit for Ana in a cute frame! There is no other explanation except that God picked Ana out a pair of glasses to restore her vision and her life. We had no idea we would be seeing Ana, but God did! In those weeks and months leading up to our trip, He set aside these glasses for our team to bring her!

It would be interesting to hear the stories of the many glasses we bring with us on the mission field! Much the same as if "these walls could talk" about old homes. Why were these particular glasses donated? Did the giver no longer need them? Have a change in vision? Simply want or need a new pair? And how did they end up in a suitcase headed for the Dominican Republic? To this particular batey?

Her vision was restored, and her right eye was no longer crossed! But in cases like this, so many miles from help and hope, her life was restored as well! She will no longer be ridiculed by other children. We are working with our church partner in Santo Domingo to be sure Ana always has a pair of glasses.

I wish I could share the video of her putting on these glasses for the first time. She sat, somber and unexpecting, looking straight ahead with her left eye while you could only see the white part of her right eye. The optometrist put on the glasses, and within two seconds her right eye turned forward and a huge smile erupted on her face! She likely saw clearly for the first time in her life! It really is miraculous when you put all the threads together as God wove, once again, a beautiful piece of His tapestry, and Ana will never forget the day her vision and life was restored by Him.

## God's Amazing Provision
*Rick Boden, MD*

Our team serves the spiritual and physical needs of the "forgotten" people of the Dominican Republic, which are Haitian migrant workers. Many of them are brought from Haiti to work in these sugar

cane villages known as bateys. Several of these Haitians have no iden-
tification papers and are, for all practical purposes, "slaves."

Throughout the week of our GHO mission trip, we met resistance
from governing authorities to provide space in each school selected
to help us see patients. Despite our desire to serve the Haitian medical needs, we were forced to utilize means other than schools or only
one or two classrooms to serve the needs of our patients.

Prior to our Thursday clinic, I performed a site visit to assess what
we could use and how to set up the next day's clinic. It was a very poor
batey, and one could "feel" the deep, pressing darkness of this batey.
As I observed the batey, I noticed goat skulls affixed upon wooden
poles indicative of active witchcraft and voodoo. I saw one worker
carrying a machete whose eyes were dark and seemed full of anger.
We left the batey and joined back with our team that evening, calling
upon our team to fervently pray as well as our prayer warrior team
members back home.

The following day, rain began to fall as we arrived at the batey.
Our team worked quickly in attempts to set up the clinic. Triage and
waiting tents quickly filled with patients, angry and impatient and demanding not to move from their spot. Tensions were high. But God....

Despite the principal of the school being warned by government
officials not to open up the neighboring school, the principle opened
the school anyway, potentially sacrificing his job to help our team
serve the local Haitians. We quickly gathered up the clinic, moved to
the school and opened up the gate of the school. The clouds parted
and the sun began to shine, and we were able safely provide the clinic.
God provided the school and cleared the rain. As a result, there were
safe working conditions both for us and our patients. Praise God and
the power of prayer!

"People will speak of the power of Your awesome acts, And I will
tell of Your greatness. They will burst forth in speaking of Your abundant goodness, And will shout joyfully of Your righteousness" (Psalm
145:6-7, NASB).

## And the Lame Will Walk
*Ann Engel, Non-medical Servant*

I was serving in the Dominican Republic with a team that had quite a few physical therapists. Our medical clinic was held in a school with no fan or air conditioning. It was a bit like practicing medicine in a sauna fully clothed! We provided general medical care, and we worked to help ease the pain of headaches, chronic neck and back pain, arthritis and Chikungunya (a mosquito-borne illness with profound joint pain). We treated many infections as well. It was pretty much a typical GHO general healthcare clinic.

Most importantly, in addition to healthcare, the evangelism aspect of our team and the local church that had a team of counselors shared the gospel of Christ with every patient who came to the clinic. Those who were already believers were asked how we could pray for them and their specific needs. God and His Holy Spirit worked on the hearts of many, and 377 people prayed to receive Christ! Not only did we try to heal or help ease pain and suffering, but the Lord was at work healing their broken souls, not just their bodies.

The real heroes on our trip were the physical therapists. While our medications will run out, their chronic pain and disabilities will last. Our physical therapy teams are a way to expand the long-term impact of our mission teams. They had team members bring wheelchairs, walkers, crutches and braces. One memorable moment was when a mother brought a 17-year-old with Cerebral Palsy who she had carried all of her life. The physical therapist reported that she was severely disabled and was not able to hold up her head by herself, much less sit or walk. Even though she could not sit, since this chair was able to recline, she was able to use it and give her mother an ability to move her daughter without carrying her. This specific wheelchair was needed for her! An ordinary wheelchair would not have worked! Another man with one leg amputated came in with the assistance of family but was able to walk out of the clinic by himself with the use of a walker provided for him.

It really did feel like seeing Jesus performing miracles with our own eyes! It was like watching Him healing and allowing the lame to walk.

## The Rest of the Story
*Joshua Daniel, RP*

The rest of the story about that God-ordained wheelchair from the previous story. I am the person who God used to bring that wheelchair with me to the Dominican Republic. After I volunteered to bring one, I had to find one. After asking around in my hometown and looking through local thrift shops to no avail, I asked my mom if she knew anyone who wanted to donate a wheelchair. She asked some folks who work in her local church office and also checked several shops. I wasn't getting anywhere until she got a text that evening from a lady at the church whose husband had called her that very day from his work at a medical facility and asked his wife if she knew anyone who needed a wheelchair because one was abandoned and was going to be thrown away.

It was a very nice chair that reclined, had a high back and had extra padding. As I prepared to get on the flight to the Dominican Republic, the airline refused to allow me to take the chair because they wanted to consider it a third bag, even though I had called ahead to let them know. After close to 30 minutes of pushing hard saying the chair had to get on the plane some way or another, they finally just made up a handmade luggage tag and sent it on.

After getting it to the Dominican Republic, I considered several times that it would be next to impossible to get a picture to share with the donor or catch whoever got the chair because I didn't work with physical therapy or go on many of the home visits this trip. On Thursday morning, I did the devotion for our group and spoke about God's sovereignty as exemplified in the story of Phillip and the Ethiopian eunuch. I related that broad principle to how He controlled every exact detail of our trip, including the specific people He would bring to the clinics, the specific times they would come and so on. And I paraphrased that we had all been brought to the Dominican Republic for such a time as this, as it is spoken in Esther.

Not long after arriving at clinic that Thursday, I decided I'd go to the restroom and then had the thought to drop by physical therapy and see how their day was starting, since we weren't too busy in pharmacy yet. Well, you guessed it! I stepped in the room and saw the chair in a reclined position and the 17-year-old girl in it. I knew immediately that it was the chair that God had ordained for the specific person He wanted to have it. I was overcome with emotion and hurried and took pictures and a short video. Everything lined up! To almost being trashed, to almost not getting on the plane, to God leading that specific mom, who had carried her child in her arms for 17 years to come to the clinic on that day, to that chair having not been given away yet, to me just "happening" to walk in that room at that exact time to see her blessed and receive the chair, God's lesson again rang truer than ever! God is sovereign over all! Praise the Lord!

## Ministry Using My Skills
*Joshua Daniel, PharmD*

It was March 2017. I was about to go to the Dominican Republic on my first short-term healthcare mission trip. Prior to the trip, I had been in a rut for a couple of years questioning what I could do to use my pharmacy skills for something other than work. One day I had a thought to check out the Christian Pharmacists Fellowship International (CPFI) website thinking they may have something for Christian pharmacists to get involved with. This led me to GHO. After some contemplating about which trip, I joined with two other pharmacists I knew and decided to go to the Dominican Republic.

That trip was atypical because there were six pharmacists and the team leader was a pharmacist. Throughout the first part of the week, I was soaking in all I was seeing. Meeting so many new people, serving so many people at clinic, seeing the sights and sounds, hearing amazing stories; it was a lot to take in. After a couple of days, my heart had really opened to seeking God and asking Him to bring the people into our paths who we were supposed to minister to and to share the good news with. Since this trip had so many pharmacists, we each had an opportunity to go on home visits. My day for home visits was Thursday, the last full day of clinic.

The local pastor took six of us a few miles from the clinic site to visit a few homes. After seeing a few patients in relatively good health that morning, I was feeling down a little because I felt we were not making much of a difference. We were told that the next home we were going to was to see a man who had an accident a few months prior. He had to have his big toe amputated because of the accident. He had an infection that was not resolving, and he got word to the pastor to ask us to come help him. So we walked several hundred yards away from the street through a lot of vegetation, and after a few minutes, I saw a house with a small porch.

We walked inside the small home and I was immediately overtaken by a putrid abscess smell that permeated the entire house. As a couple of us walked into the bedroom, I saw Alejandro, a man in his early 40s, laying there with his leg bandaged. After we spoke to him, the doctor wanted to unwrap the bandage and evaluate his leg. So, he limped from the bed to outside on the porch so we all could attend to him. As the bandages were removed, I was shocked to see this man's condition. From the shin down there was massive infection and extreme necrosis. A lot of skin was gone, and the tendons and muscles were all in plain sight. He had several gaping holes in his foot that oozed puss and infection. My heart sank as I saw this man not even flinch at the dangerous condition he was in. I thought to myself that never in the U.S. would someone be in this condition and just sit there. He was in an extremely dangerous condition and could develop sepsis or lose his leg. We were all shocked! The doctor and medical student began to clean his leg with some betadine that he had stored in a 20-ounce Coca Cola bottle and then rebandaged it with new dressing and gauze. We gave him the only antibiotics we had in our bag of medications.

While this interaction was unfolding on his porch, I looked a few yards away across the yard and saw our physical therapist holding a teenage girl around her waist like a bear hug trying to get her out of a wheelchair to assess her mobility. My understanding was the girl had possibly overdosed on some medication in a possible suicide attempt and was now a triplegic. These simultaneous dueling sights broke me as compassion took over my heart. I stepped back a few feet from the others and tears flowed. I had a thought during that moment that these events were probably remarkably similar to what Jesus encountered as he traveled throughout Israel. He went from town to town and home to home and ministered to those who were suffering physically and spiritually. He often provided miraculous physical healing, helped the lame to walk, healed the lepers and even raised some from the dead, but most importantly he offered the good news of eternal life. We offered what limited physical help we could to these two, but we also offered love, shared the good news and prayed with them and their families.

After the trip ended, I arrived home a changed person. The God sightings from that day confirmed my calling to serve in this capacity. It taught me about God's sovereignty. He led me and our group specifically to those two people to share about His love. That day impacted me so much that within a week of returning and processing everything, I decided that I needed to return as soon as possible. I signed up for the next trip, which was a couple months later. I continued to branch out to more trips and locations and will soon lead a team. I fully realized serving with GHO and the mission they stand for, to serve others and to share the good news with others through healthcare missions, was something I was called to do.

As a follow-up to further display God's sovereignty, I returned to the Dominican Republic on another trip two years later. The latter half of the week we moved to another site. As the bus pulled up to the second site, I immediately realized it was the same site we had gone to on my first trip. I could not believe I was there again. The sights all came rushing back to my mind. I remembered everything.

I finally had a little break on the first day in the afternoon and I saw Carlos, the local pastor. I quickly walked over to him and greeted him and asked how things were going in his community since I had last been there. Then I asked, "Carlos, do you remember Alejandro? Do you know how he fared after we left?" I told him how I had prayed for him many times over the last two years. His answer stunned me. He exclaimed, "Joshua! He was here at the clinic today; he was here maybe 30 minutes ago." He immediately started searching and looking for him at the clinic to reconnect us. Unfortunately, he had already left and gone home. I was disappointed I did not get to see him, but the joy of knowing he was alive and doing much better and was part of the ministry thrilled me.

These events strengthened my faith and confirmed my calling to go and help others with healthcare and to share the good news of Jesus.

## Never Too Old
### David Molind, PA

It is not too unusual for people to travel long distances to be seen at one of our medical clinics. Many may walk long hours and literally sole wearing distances to be seen. Riding a horse to our Dominican clinic is a little more extraordinary; however, this was not to be the only extraordinary event to transpire that heat-drenched afternoon.

The man trotted his horse near to the gate and slowly, carefully and yet somewhat awkwardly dismounted the horse and tied it to a nearby tree. Unassumingly, he made his way to register and check in. Beneath the brim of his black brimmed hat was a weathered face of a relatively quiet, slight man wearing the smartest clothes he had as a sign of respect for the doctor he hoped to see.

As he slowly but intentionally moved his way, in the heat of afternoon sun, through the clinic from check in to triage to reach his anticipated goal, he demanded no attention. When he reached his goal of being seen by the doctor, the tables began to turn. The man who had worn his best clothes as a sign of respect for another quickly drew the respect of the doctor. It was not that he came by himself, or that he was not taking any medications, or that he had not been seen by a doctor in any recent memory, but that the man revealed he had more years on this earth than degrees Fahrenheit of that sweltering hot day!

A total of 111 birthdays had passed in his life. He had asked for an exam to make sure he was of good health! By physical exam he appeared to be so. After pleasant conversation and prayer for his extended good health and safe travel home, he was dispatched to counseling with a newfound entourage attending to his needs. In his private time at counseling, he asked to know more about who Jesus is. A spirit-led church member led him to Christ, and he made a profession of faith after 111 years of walking without the light of life, 111 years of waiting for someone to care, share and prepare him for the light of Christ to enter his life.

Pharmacy celebrated his decision for Christ and gave him the only thing the doctor ordered, a multivitamin and acetaminophen. By all accounts he did appear a weathered man as would we all, had we spent over a century without the way, the truth and the light. Hopping up on a brick wall he was able to mount his horse, and together they slowly trotted down the crimson clay road in a new knowledge and new family together in Christ.

He came dressed out of respect for others, but in the end he left clothed in the love of Jesus Christ and respect from others.

## The Right Person, Place and Time
*Carolyn Grosvenor, MD*

On my first trip to the Dominican Republic, we served in a Haitian batey (a shantytown or camp where sugarcane cutters live). This trip was different in that I often needed two translators! I spoke English to the Dominican translator, who then translated into Spanish for the second translator, who then translated into Haitian Creole for my patient. And then, they would retrace the whole process back to me.

One day I went out to the waiting area to get a patient. I made eye contact with a tall man to come with me. When he stood up, I saw he could barely walk. He had to lean on me to get to my examination station. My head barely came above his shoulders.

He came to the clinic because of a painful right knee. Besides pain, his knee often gave out on him. I think he was in his 50s or 60s. Working in the cane fields is long, hard work. He worked more than 12 hours a day. I think I forgot where I was when I asked him why he worked so many hours! He simply said: "I have to eat."

I knew naproxen and analgesic rub weren't going to enable him to work 12 hours in the field, but maybe a brace would help. So, I went to our physical therapist to see if she had a brace that would fit him. Now, on this trip, several of our crates were held up in customs for a couple of days. It turns out that the crate with the braces arrived at the clinic just the day before my patient came to the clinic. And she had only one type of brace that would suit him.

I went back and retrieved my tall gentleman and helped him hobble over to the physical therapist. She put the brace on his leg and adjusted the straps, and then he stood up and took a step. The smile on his face broke my heart!! Oh, my goodness. I felt like shouting and having a hallelujah moment! I watched as he strutted across the road to get his naproxen and analgesic rub from the pharmacy. It was like a John Wayne strut!

In the U.S. he would have been referred for surgery, but he is not in the U.S. A simple brace changed his quality of life and saved his life. As he said, "I have to eat."

I do believe the Lord goes before us and orchestrates things so the right person is at the right place at the right time so He can pour out His blessing. My patient made it to the clinic on the day after the crate arrived with the one brace he needed.

During my first few trips with GHO, I was often overwhelmed by the need and distressed by the number of people we were not able to serve. However, I have since learned to focus on the person the Lord puts in front of me. I believe every encounter on the mission field is divinely appointed, not just for the benefit of my patient but for the Lord's glory. The transformation from a distressed man who could barely walk to one with a huge grin and a John Wayne strut warms my heart even to this day. This is why I continue to go on GHO mission trips.

## Why Do I Keep Going?
*Rick Schurman, PT*

We had been in the clinic four days and I was starting to wonder, "Why? Why do I keep going and serving?" The Dominican Republic is hot in July, and we were working in an abandoned music school in an area of Santo Domingo, San Christóbal. This area had been at one time a nice section of town before being hit by a hurricane in the 1980s. Since that time, many of the homes were now shacks with metal sides and no electricity or running water.

Our three physical therapists were part of a large team that was averaging some 800 patients per day. Lines of hundreds of patients greeted us each morning when we arrive on the bus. The team included physicians, dentists, optometrists, pharmacists and nurses, in addition to several family members who assist in the different areas of the clinic. Our national team, Oasis Church, also supplied up to 150 volunteers as well.

The physical therapists had been busy all week seeing a variety of usual conditions, including back and neck pain and orthopedic injuries. However, this year we also had some unusual cases. Thursday was a usual day until I saw a 97-year-old man for back pain. He seemed to do well with the treatment I had suggested, and then he told me his story. He had 27 children with the same wife. He was now living with his 60-year-old son who had fallen out of a fruit tree 20 years earlier and had a lower C-spine fracture. He had been a quadriplegic ever since. The father, who was his only caregiver, was wondering if I had a wheelchair to give him for his son. I told him with tears in my eyes that we had given all our wheelchairs away the day before. We had transferred five chairs down with the team, but they go very quickly due to the tremendous needs. I felt horrible. I felt even worse that I had not thought about taking down his name and address to try and send one back.

On Friday morning, I went out with the final home visit team. All week the team had been sending out these smaller teams consisting of a physical therapist, physician, nurse, translator and pastor to go into the homes of those too sick to travel to the clinic. We went along the river and watched the local boys swimming in the brown water. There was garbage on the banks of the river with goats going through the garbage enjoying their lunch. The people were wonderful and so appreciative. The children were beautiful. The conditions were disgusting.

As I ducked to go into the last home prior to returning to the clinic, my heart seemed to skip a beat. I saw in the small two-room house the 97-year-old man and his son. The son was sitting in a high back wooden chair. We greeted each other and I shared my story quickly with the home visit team. We were all amazed and thankful God had brought us to this home for the last home visit. As I stood there, I looked over the floor area. I saw groove marks in the floor from the wooden chair being dragged from one room to the other. My emotions were raw. What dedication for the elderly man to care for his son for 20 years in this condition!

After this trip, our daughter decided to return to Santo Domingo to teach. We sent a wheelchair back with her, and a few weeks later, I was blessed to see the pictures of them receiving the chair.

Our work in the clinic or hospital every day offers us great opportunities to change people's lives. We facilitate the healing process; we give people their function back and help them live better. There are few times in life that it gets any better than literally changing the life of our patient. Each time my life changes also. This is why. This is why I keep going.

# ECUADOR
## 1.8312° S, 78.1834° W

## Be a Servant
*Charles Bruerd, DO*

I was serving on a small team to Ecuador with one physician, two nurse practitioners, three medical students, a pharmacist and a few logistical servant helpers. We were serving in a small bedroom community of South Quito. We were working alongside two national physicians and a dentist from the local church who had agreed to join our team. It is always a beautiful picture of the body of Christ to have people working side by side who do not even speak the same language and are from two different cultures. Just a little taste of heaven!

Each mission trip is different, and this one was just that. We had a focus for the week on servanthood and what it means to be a true servant. During our week, this small team saw 1,500 patients. We were busy! Our teams usually pray with and/or share the gospel with each patient we see. Because we were a small team and had so many patients waiting, we referred each patient to a national team member for spiritual counseling.

As each patient visited the spiritual counseling area, they sat down with a local church member. These servants initiated a conversation with the patients by asking all of them the same question, "How can I pray for you today?" They really responded to the chance to connect with the local church members who worked and lived among them every day. God was glorified in that 750 souls came to a saving grace during that hectic week! What a blessing to see God take what this small team had to offer to magnify His kingdom!

We always have a final team meeting on our mission trips. This is the team's chance to reflect on the week and all the Lord has done in and through our team. We gathered together for the last time this very team would likely ever be together again. We had a special moment as one of the team members read from the Scriptures as the team leader and I washed the feet of the local pastor and the head national doctor of the clinic. Countless tears were shed that day as we reflected on what Jesus was sent here for—to serve and not be served. We closed the gathering by providing each team member with a small towel as a symbol for doing what our Lord instructed us to do, to be a servant and not one who is served.

## Blessed with Crutches
*Nate Bernard, MDiv*

We had a GHO team one year serving in southern Ecuador. One of the most common complaints we see on our mission trips is neck and back pain or joint pain from a mild to severe injury or any type of arthritis. These patients do not typically have any pain medications, not even a common over the counter acetaminophen or ibuprofen. They don't typically have any sort of splint or brace, crutches or wheelchair. And rarely would they have a prosthetic.

An elderly man came into our clinic complaining that his left knee was hurting. He was seen by a nurse practitioner who was with us. She rolled up his left pant leg to examine his knee that was hurting. It was inflamed and had some lateral bowing to it, with some arthritis as well. She asked if she could roll up the right pant leg to compare his knees. And there it was—a homemade wooden peg leg right out of Pirates of the Caribbean!

He had to tie this wood prosthetic on every morning with leather straps! He had had the same homemade wood prosthetic since 1964, after a tree had fallen on his ankle and crushed it, requiring it to be amputated. He had been using a cane in his right hand, which caused additional strain on his left leg.

Fortunately, on many of our teams we have physical therapists who bring along a variety of donated splints, braces, crutches and walkers or wheelchairs. We did have our physical therapist get involved, who provided him with a new pair of forearm crutches. He was also able to show him how to properly use these crutches. Before he left the clinic, he was walking with much more ease and much less pain. Our teams now bring prosthetic hands for above and below the elbow amputations, but legs are much more difficult. A leg prosthetic would require exact pre-measurements and is designed for each person individually, thus rendering this impossible for our mission teams until we are able to make them in-country. Still, crutches made a huge difference in his ability to walk.

God showed up in this man's life on this day through a new pair of crutches. His freedom to go where he wanted was restored. He was so grateful! The ironic thing is he is a woodworker by trade. No, he did not make his wooden leg.

## Body of Christ
*Bob Coulter, RPh*

My first few mission teams were to Ecuador with our national partners, Tammy, Marilyn and the Verbo Church. Over the years we have served in many different areas of Ecuador. It is a beautiful country!

One day I had a doctor come to the pharmacy asking for catheters and lubricant. She had a mother with a young adult daughter who was paralyzed and needed to be catheterized as she was too large for her mother to move when she needed to void. She had apparently contracted a viral infection when she was a little girl that left her paralyzed, and she had been cared for by her parents for more than 10 years. The dad worked in the fields so he was not available to move the girl to a place where she could relieve herself, likely not a bathroom anyway.

Our teams bring in all our medications and supplies for our week of clinic. Sometimes we can leave some behind that won't expire for us to use on our next mission trip, but these types of supplies are not common, and we likely would not have them. In this case, we didn't have any catheters or lubricant, so the doctor explained this to the mother. She then began to share that what she really wanted was to just take her daughter's life then her own and put an end to this very longstanding and difficult family situation. Could you imagine her hopelessness?

The doctor came to me with this information, and I remembered I had seen a large transport chair (small wheels and a molded rigid seat) in the supply room in Cuenca, our host's home base. Tammy was able to arrange for bus transport of the chair, which arrived in a couple days. This would allow her mother to help transfer her daughter for bathroom needs. After returning home, I was later able to get a wheelchair for them through the Joni & Friends ministry.

The following year, the family brought her to the team and thanked us for all we had done. God is able to do what we think of as impossible! Much like feeding 5,000 with just a couple of fish and a few loaves of bread, He took a need, gave our team the inspiration to help in a way different than the original request and then used other ministries to participate and provide the wheelchair. It was the body of Christ, working together around the world. It is truly a pleasure and privilege to serve Him through healthcare and to watch as He works through His people.

## Eternal Healing
### *Kelly Stanek Wigglesworth, Medical Student*

As a fresh-out-of-first-year medical student, I was overjoyed to serve on the GHO mission trip to Pasaje, Ecuador. On the third day of our clinic, I headed over to the physical therapy and orthopedic area to help where I could with my minimal knowledge but great excitement. Our team was blessed to have an orthopedic surgeon, Dr. Curt, who occasionally gave injections for osteoarthritis. I always marveled at the fact that these steroid injections were sometimes elixirs of life for patients crippled by their stenotic joints. However, on this day we met a young woman who had injured her hand in a car accident quite a while ago. She reported continued severe pain in her right hand, which interfered with her ability to work and afford a local doctor.

Luckily, Dr. Curt noticed that though the surface of the hand had healed from the car accident, he could palpate a foreign object lodged in the tendon. Together, we prepared the woman for the procedure, which was a small surgery we prayed would make a large impact. Dr. Curt excised the piece of glass, which was restricting the passage of the tendons of multiple fingers. After suturing and bandaging the hand, we prayed with her for her physical and spiritual health, asking God to rain down on this seed of healing and let it prosper. Teary-eyed she thanked us, giving all of us hugs and kisses.

After the prayers and gratitude, I noticed a golden glimmer on her neck. I complimented her necklace, a beautiful pearl pendant with a gold chain. She immediately took it off and gifted it to me. Overwhelmed, tears welled in my eyes—I could not imagine the sacrifice it was to give such a lovely gift. I remembered I was wearing a silver cross necklace from home and quickly took it off to give it to her. She took my necklace and said, "This way I will always remember you, your kindness and Jesus." I said that with her necklace I will always remember and pray for her. I do not know the story behind her golden pearl necklace, but it was a glimpse into the mind of this sweet woman— how she was more grateful than I imagined for a simple surgery. I pray God blesses her hand with complete healing and the cross necklace reminds her that God is the true, eternal healer of both body and soul.

## God Sees the Need
*Marilyn Guido, RN*
*National Partner, Ecuador*

After hosting GHO teams for more than 20 years, I could tell so many stories, but this is one of my favorites. We were taking a team to work in the town of Santa Rosa on the southern coast of Ecuador. The local pastor's wife was working with the mayor's office in a program to help people who were begging on the streets. They would go walking, and when they found a beggar, they would ask to go to their homes where they could see what the situation was and what help could be given. It seems they were always calling me asking for wheelchairs, which I can only get when a healthcare mission team comes down.

On this particular team, one of the doctor's wives had a friend who worked in a storeroom of donated items in Alaska. Could you get any further from Ecuador? She called Beth and said, "Why don't you come by and see what you'd like to take on your mission trip?" Beth decided, among other things, to bring 11 (yes, 11) wheelchairs. She carefully wrapped them all in plastic and talked to her friends at Alaska Airlines where she had worked for a time, and they booked all 11 wheelchairs through to Guayaquil for no cost! That would have been enough of a miracle right there, but the Ecuador pastor's wife gave me a list of the people they found who needed a wheelchair. There were 11 names!

We decided to have a little ceremony to present the new wheel-chairs to the happy recipients. We held the list, and looked at each chair, and taped a person's name to it. When we got to the last chair and unwrapped it, it was missing a foot piece! We were so sad that this last person would not get a complete chair. We looked high and low through all the supplies that were brought down and never found the foot piece.

All the people gathered at our clinic site for the ceremony, people from the mayor's office, the newspapers and the local TV station were there. We called out the names, and the people came forward one by one, and it seemed like each chair was fitted exactly for that person. It was just amazing. We finally got to the last person. After we called his name, an elderly gentleman was brought forward in the rickety chair he had been using. As we transferred him to his new chair, ready to apologize for the lack of a leg piece, we realized that same leg had been amputated! He didn't need a leg piece on that side!

What a blessing for us as the national partner with GHO for Ecuador and our local hosts to have that strong confirmation from the Lord! That He sees the needs and forms the plan from about as far away as possible, and we get to see it all come together. Every team we are privileged to host has clear evidence that God has been working on our behalf, long before they arrive. As we pray, we are always excited to see how the week will unfold. At times it seems we have strong opposition. From getting permission from the government, making some kind of arrangements like changing the clinic site days before the team arrives, finding out the cook moved out of town, fun stuff! Just some kind of wrench in the gear. When that happens, we feel an overwhelming peace. If the devil is trying to bring on that kind of battle, it is only because the Lord is preparing mighty, supernatural fruit from the service and love the team is bringing.

## Mentoring the Next Generation
### *Lloyd DeFoor, Non-medical Servant*

I have been tremendously blessed to serve with so many outstanding young people over the years. It is a special blessing to encourage and mentor the students and young professionals who serve on our mission teams. I have seen many young people decide to go to medical school, nursing school, dental school or pharmacy school after serving with us on trips. This includes those on our teams as well as those serving alongside our team working with our national partners on the mission field. Often our national partner is a church, and many in the church pitch in and help while GHO is in country running the medical campaign. It can take a lot of volunteers to make our medical clinics a success!

Some of our partner churches allow students in the church to serve as interpreters as part of their school program. They get experience and practice with their English as well as mentoring by our team. Over the years, many of them have chosen a medical career after serving with our team. Our mission trips open the eyes of many, even if they don't become long-term missionaries, to use their career as a ministry, even at home.

I have also had the privilege to serve with a number of people who have become full-time missionaries as well after experiencing the joy of serving others around the world. Years ago, Meghan and Caitlin went with us to Ecuador. Meghan was a young student doctor and Caitlin was a nurse. On this trip, God worked in their hearts and lives, and they have since devoted their lives to serving in a small, poor village in Bolivia. They are difference makers in the lives of the people they serve. They have been on the frontlines during the COVID-19 pandemic, and they do everything from delivering babies to looking after all the different ailments we see on our trips. GHO helped these two young ladies get it. Their lives are full of so much joy because of serving the Lord and His children. They did not settle for the good life they could have had in the United States. They are experiencing the great life that comes with a life of service that advances the kingdom.

## A Shattered Crystal Ceiling
*Bob Coulter, RPh*

A few years ago, I had dinner with friends in a neighboring community who had invited others to join us for dinner. During the meal, my travel with GHO on foreign healthcare mission trips came up as a topic of conversation. One woman showed a great deal of interest in what we did on the teams. She was a 30-something massage therapist and very outgoing and mature.

The next day God moved me to contact her with an offer for her to go on the team and I would cover her expenses. She was surprised but eager to go! On our mission trips, there is a strong spiritual focus, and the team preparation begins with devotions emailed to the team long before they are ready to leave. During the mission trip, we have morning and evening praise and worship, as well as a devotion and/or testimony, typically done by different team members throughout the week. The team devotions challenged her concept of God and the truth of the gospel. She claimed to have no trouble with the concept of God the Father or with the Holy Spirit (being very spiritual herself), but the idea of Jesus was a major stumbling block. All of Him. His divinity, His sacrifice, His miracles, etc. were all incomprehensible. And the idea that He was the ONLY way to heaven was completely off her chart.

I assigned a mature former teammate to stay close to her, and we made it through the week. In clinic, she was a star. She organized the non-medical servants on the team like an experienced team leader. We had traveled together to and from the same departure city, so we talked some more on the way home but didn't come to any resolution of her issues.

I dropped her off late Saturday night at a friend's house as she still had a one-and-a-half-hour drive to her home. Sometime later I found out that she didn't sleep well and left early so she could get to church back home. When she got to church, the message was on Luke 12:9 where Jesus says, "But he who denies Me before men will be denied before the angels of God" (NKJV). Her crystal ceiling (her name was actually Crystal!) was shattered and she received Christ as her Savior and Lord. I see her occasionally and know she continues to follow Him.

This reminds me that spiritual growth of the team needs to be continually regarded along with those we are caring for, including our patients, national church and team and those God puts in our path such as the hotel staff or people who help prepare and serve our meals. We are there to show the love of Christ in a real, tangible way through healthcare, but also in other ways as the Lord provides opportunity. And of course, this focus helps to teach us to do this at home and not just when we leave for another country "on mission." We are always on mission.

## Serve Him
*Matthew Montgomery, MD*

Each night, after another day of repairing hernias and removing gall bladders, I would drive my fancy car home to my big, perfectly landscaped house to slouch down into my sofa. I would sit and blankly stare at my big screen TV. Sometimes I wouldn't even bother to turn it on. I was physically, emotionally and spiritually exhausted from the stress of long hours, never-ending patient demands and crushing lawsuits. I was painfully realizing that lots of money and possessions did not bring the joy I had anticipated. My spiritual life was diminished to nothing more than a monthly church service where I usually fell asleep. I was once again falling into a deep depression. I even had thoughts of suicide. My life and career were empty and meaningless.

During these dark times, I struggled to answer two questions. First, for whom was I practicing medicine? My patients didn't appreciate my work; it seemed as though they were lining up to sue me. My wife thought I would be happier if I quit. I was miserable. And secondly, why did I even have this knowledge and skills? Why bother? I was ready to give them up and at the end of my rope.

Fortunately, this was just before I was scheduled to go on a GHO healthcare mission trip to Ecuador. I had been before, and this mission trip had become the highlight of my year. I longed for the chance to join with GHO and serve the needs of truly needy people. I also longed for the fellowship, teamwork and camaraderie with our medical team and national partners. I loved the morning and evening worship time and devotions. And it was all in the name of furthering God's kingdom and in the heaven-like natural beauty of Ecuador. I always returned home from these trips with a fresh, new perspective on life.

I was very nervous before my first mission trip with GHO. My prayers centered on not being eaten by a cannibal, dying of malaria or killing a patient in the wilds of the jungle. This trip, however, proved to be different and truly life changing. With a little experience already under my belt, this trip my prayers were asking God to "awaken me spiritually." Little did I know what I was in for!

About halfway through our trip, while in the dining area of our hotel high in the Andes Mountains, God answered my prayers. And I mean literally. For the first and only time in my life, I heard God speak to me, just as if He was in the chair next to me. He said, "Matt, thank you for coming to Ecuador to serve me. I do appreciate it. But, Matt, the reason I gave you your surgical skills and abilities is to serve me every day...right where you live. You don't have to travel to a different continent to serve me."

I was astonished! I suddenly understood. That's it! I thought. My questions were answered. God gave me my abilities and talents to SERVE HIM! But how? I remembered reading about an oncologist who offered to pray with his patients. I found that fascinating but knew I couldn't do that in a secular practice. My partners wouldn't stand for it. Well, right then and there, I decided to try it, regardless of the outcome.

After returning home, I began to offer to pray for my patients in the office, emergency room and operating room. I was definitely on to something. I saw a light to my darkness. Very quickly, however, the problem of making this work in my secular practice was solved. I was "released" from the practice in which I had been so low and miserable. I left that meeting and kicked my heels together in joy! I had no idea where I was going to practice or even live, but I knew I was going to serve the Lord and make my practice a ministry for Jesus.

In the next few months, God practically "parted the Red Sea" in knocking down barriers and obstacles in facilitating the founding of my new solo general surgery practice, Cornerstone Surgical. From the cross on the front door and business cards to the Christian art and Scripture on the waiting room walls, to my offering to pray for all my patients—my practice is different. I now use my skills and knowledge to bring glory to Jesus. I have a new meaning in life and use what God has given me to lead people to the Lord. God has used my practice beyond what I thought was possible. My emptiness and depression have been replaced with purpose and fulfillment. I serve Him out of deep gratitude for all He has done. It doesn't get much better than that!

## Your Heart Not Mine
*Meghan Scott, MD*
*with Caitlin Lawrence, RN, BSN*

As a fourth year medical student anxious about graduating and starting family medicine residency, I had no idea "what I wanted to do with my life" after residency. I knew family medicine was the right specialty for me, and I was convinced healthcare could be used as a means to ministry, but I did not know what that might look like after finishing my training. One of my physician mentors from CMDA encouraged me to use my available elective time to do a short-term medical mission trip, but little did he know how God would use that trip to change my heart.

As my mother is originally from Chile, I have always had one foot in Latino culture and have always had a special place in my heart for Latin America. Therefore, when looking through GHO's trip calendar, the decision to go to Santa Isabel, Ecuador was simple. My best friend and fellow healthcare worker, Caitlin, jumped at the opportunity to go with me as, unknown to me at the time, she had been praying for an opportunity to use her nursing skills abroad for a while.

When I look back and see how God used that trip to change my heart and life, I can see that the transformation started well before I ever set foot in Ecuador. As my fellow teammates and I began preparing months in advance, we read through John Piper's *Let the Nations Be Glad!* Through reading this book, God began to show me His heart for the nations, and as I studied God's Word leading up to the trip, I felt God shaping my heart to be more like His.

Once we arrived in Ecuador and began seeing patients in Santa Isabel, I was blown away with how well healthcare and faith can be used together. I began to understand more clearly that my role as a physician extends well beyond physical healing and includes spiritual and emotional healing as well. That anxiety and uncertainty about my life after residency slipped away, and I felt at peace caring for others in the hopes of making God's name great in Ecuador. I felt a stirring in my heart to go and use medicine to bring the hope of physical and spiritual healing to those who have not heard.

Our final night in Santa Isabel was a night of worship with our partnering local church and patients we had seen that week. As we all came together to worship the Lord, I was struck once again by the beauty of God's universal church. As our team sang in English alongside the Ecuadorian voices in Spanish, I was reminded of God's desire to be known throughout the world. His desire for every nation, tribe and tongue to know Him and to worship Him. His unquenched zeal for His own glory and for our good.

I left Santa Isabel with a newfound desire to go to the nations. Returning to the U.S., I graduated from medical school, started residency and began praying about what this new calling might mean for my life. I prayed for confirmation from the Lord, and He provided it by allowing me to return to Ecuador with GHO the following year. After this second trip, I knew in my heart that I was being called to long-term healthcare missions.

As somewhat of a homebody, it was quite a surprise to my family to hear that I wanted to serve as a long-term healthcare missionary. They questioned if I was sure about my decision, as I have never wanted to be far away from my friends and family in North Carolina. I understood their concern as it did seem out of character for myself, but my only explanation was that the Holy Spirit had worked in my heart. The Holy Spirit had changed me and given me the desire to go, and I wanted to be obedient.

Interestingly enough, Caitlin also felt God working in her own heart and whispering to her to go to the nations. We began to seek out mission agencies and opportunities and were eventually led to speak with SIM. Despite going through the application process separately and not asking to be sent together, the mission decided to send us as a team, physician and nurse, to Potosí, Bolivia.

Now eight years after that initial trip to Santa Isabel, Caitlin and I have been serving in Bolivia for three and a half years. We have had the opportunity to care for families in the family medicine clinic Allinta

## GOD SIGHTINGS

Ruwana (Quechua for "doing good"), deliver babies, pray for healing, hold the hands of dying hospice patients, teach residents and recently graduated nurses and physicians, and, most importantly, share the love of Christ through healthcare. It has not been easy, and there have been many days where I have been acutely aware of my own inadequacy and my need for God's grace and strength daily.

We never imagined battling a global pandemic, leading to the collapse of the local healthcare system in our town, but we trusted that if God called us to be here, He would equip us and sustain us. We knew God had been preparing us, even while in the mountains of Ecuador eight years ago, for such a time as this.

# EL SALVADOR

13.7942° N, 88.8965° W

## Disciples Making Disciples
*Pastor Mauricio Barrientos*
*National Partner, El Salvador*

My name is Pastor Mauricio, I am Salvadorian and work as one of the pastors at Oasis Church here in El Salvador. We have been blessed to have been partnering with GHO for more than 20 years now. GHO has been so wonderful to us! GHO has been used by our Lord to help us to have a new vision on how to approach entire communities in our country.

We have been receiving medical teams for years, with our churches doing several medical campaigns each year. We have moved all around our country, and these medical campaigns help us to extend our outreach into new communities with the gospel of Christ. We have done several church plants in our country, frequently with the help of a GHO team in reaching out to people in different areas.

Many of the students in our schools are able to help serve as interpreters for the GHO teams, and they are able to practice their English language. It is a huge blessing for them, and we often have more volunteers from our church than are needed to serve. Many of these students have been loved on and mentored through the love of Christ that is in the doctors, nurses and others serving on the team. One of the most impacting fruits of all these years of serving together is that now, after many years of working with GHO mission teams to help our people, many of these students have gone on to become healthcare professionals. All from watching the team demonstrate loving others and God by serving Him through healthcare.

We had been scheduled to host a team in a particular area of El Salvador where we were hoping to plant a church several times. The first time we changed the location of the team because we were wanting a large team to come and allow us to serve this area, but it was a smaller team, so we chose to delay until the next year. The next year a much larger team was recruited, and we were excited to reach this area, but COVID-19 changed all of these plans as this mission trip was cancelled. We rescheduled for the following spring and again, a team was recruited by GHO, but due to ongoing issues with COVID-19 and a return quarantine required, this mission trip was cancelled once again.

After much prayer, we felt the Lord was urging us to proceed with our plans to reach this area. COVID-19 has been hard on our country, and we didn't want to delay trying to reach this area that had a lot of witchcraft and false doctrines being taught. So, we proceeded with plans to run a medical campaign using only our national physicians, dentists, nurses, etc. Our church helped with the logistical non-medical servant roles as well as with evangelism. We used the model of a GHO medical campaign. They were kind enough to let us use all the medications we had stored in our country and donated some funds toward buying additional medications, plus we raised some funds on our own as well. The beauty of this campaign is that many of the physicians, dentists and nurses were those same students who had served with GHO teams years before. It was precious!

The medical campaign was very successful, and on our last day of clinic we found a family given by the Lord! They have opened their home to start church meetings every Saturday afternoon. Just like Lydia at Ephesus with apostle Paul! We are so excited with the joy His gratitude produces. Hallelujah! This is the definition of success for short-term missions. Praise God!

## Is This the One?
*Hannah Chow-Johnson, MD*

My children played youth soccer, so we had an abundance of soccer balls. I brought three of them with me to El Salvador for our mission trip to use in the children's ministry. Shouts of excitement echoed through the military base as children played while we saw patients, preached the gospel and ran a children's program in the courtyard. Sometimes it was hard to hear because of all the goings on. One time, I had to completely halt what I was doing due to one of the volunteers praising God and fronting a conga line followed by many loudly screaming excited children and the simultaneous thwacking of rotors due to helicopters taking off and landing. I stopped examining the patient, smiled at the mom and her children, and we all giggled as we settled down to listen and wait.

The week flew by quickly. On Friday, I talked with Jessica, a fellow team doctor, about giving away the soccer balls. We shared a clinic space, with the partition kept partially open so we could talk. One of our balls had been promised to one of our volunteers, so I told Jessica we each could give away a ball. We prayed before clinic started, as was our custom, that the Lord would let us know which children should receive a ball.

With every patient I saw that day, I would ask the Lord, "Lord, is this the one?" Then one young teen stepped into my cubicle. As we talked, I asked him what his favorite sport was. "Fútbol" was the reply. No surprise as soccer was hands down the most popular sport among the children we saw in the clinic. "¿Tienes una pelota?" Do you have a ball? "No, solo no lo tengo." No, I don't. Then I felt the Lord say, "He is the one." Exactly at the same time, Jessica turned around from her cubicle, pointed at the boy and said, "He's the one." He and his mother were delighted and surprised when I offered him the ball. He told me he and his cousins had a plastic ball to play soccer with, but it wasn't the same.

"When you play soccer, I pray you will remember that God has given you a much better gift, the gift of salvation through His son Jesus," I said, looking him in the eye. He nodded. I still am in awe that He considered the gift of the ball so important that He made sure I knew this boy was the one He chose. I am humbly reminded that I need to always listen for His still, small voice, and that He speaks through other Christians in our lives. I don't know what plans the Lord has for this young patient, but I pray the Lord will use him—and maybe the soccer ball too.

## The Right Wrong Bus
### *Bryan Stoudt, MDiv*

I was serving in El Salvador, and on one of our clinic days a 12-year-old boy checked in by himself. While it is unheard of here in the U.S., it is not that uncommon for children, especially older ones, to come alone to our clinics. We registered him and then sent him to triage. At triage, he was not able to give a physical complaint or reason for his visit. When he was sent to the medical team and was able to see a physician and did not have any real physical concerns, the physician was able to get him talking to try and find out why he had come to a medical clinic.

It turned out he had never intended to come to our clinic at all. Earlier that day, he had boarded a bus, thinking it was heading to the beach as part of the new mayor's initiatives at the beginning of his tenure. Apparently, a large portion of the poor have never seen the beach, so as a matter of goodwill, the new mayor provided free bus rides to the beach for many to have a chance to see the beach. He had gotten on the wrong bus and found himself at the GHO clinic site instead. Can you imagine his initial disappointment?

The physician who saw this boy learned he had run away from home, at just 10 years old, to join a gang. Gangs are a real and serious problem in El Salvador. Children are recruited at a young age and are at risk of being hurt or killed if they refuse to join a gang. There is also the threat to their own family if they refuse. So, many of these young boys join gangs long before they are ready to face a harsh world. The physician wisely asked the local pastor they were serving with to engage with him to see how they could help.

Unbeknownst to anyone, his mother "just happened" to be there that day, too, to receive the free healthcare we were offering. This momma had not seen her son since he had run away from home two years ago! As you can imagine, she was overjoyed to see him again!

Unfortunately, the son was not willing to come home with her. He was probably scared of gang retaliation. He was, however, able to visit with his mom and together with the pastor and his mom prayed for reconciliation. Who knows what God may do?

## Through You and In You
*Lori Koon, RN*

While I was on a GHO trip to El Salvador, I was assigned to a group doing home visits on Monday afternoon. At the last home we visited, a 76-year-old lady sat in her wheelchair on the porch. I felt an instant connection to this precious lady. She was using a wheelchair due to arthritis in her hips. She could walk but needed a lot of support to do so, and she did not have access to a walker. During the visit, the afternoon rain intensified, so her wide porch roof enabled us to have a longer visit with her as we waited for the rain to ease up.

When I returned to the clinic, I asked a teammate if he knew if there were any walkers available. He told me that's what was in the boxes he brought along from Pennsylvania. One was then set aside for this lady.

I was thinking of her and praying for her the next morning. I wanted to share Isaiah 41:10 with her and encourage her, but I knew it would be another teammate's turn to go on the visits that day, so I wrote out the verse, "Do not fear, for I am with you; Do not be afraid, for I am your God. I will strengthen you, I will also help you, I will also uphold you with My righteous right hand" (ESV). I wrote it on a card and asked the other nurse to give it to the lady. God orchestrated the details, and somehow, I was allowed to go on the visit to this lady's house that day as well. The interpreter with me was also excited because God was giving her a joy and desire to do the home visits. What a blessing it was to be able to encourage this woman and see her start walking with the support she needed. Her daughter was there, and with tears in her eyes, she told us this was the most she had seen her mother walk in years. The pastor prayed for her. Then God prompted me to share an instruction for walker use that I used to hear the physical therapists say frequently to patients where I had previously worked. After returning to the clinic, I told a teammate about that odd, sudden prompting. She replied, "I wouldn't have known to tell her that." Just an example of how God can use all of our past experiences to be of service to others at some point in time.

Later that week at an evening church service, the lady's sister came to church. She said she decided to come because of all of the kindness that had been shown to her family.

Two years later, I was in the same city of El Salvador with GHO. Clinic days can get busy, and the eyeglasses station is a popular place. One afternoon, I was assigned to this area. I can speak some Spanish but am certainly not fluent. Knowing I would need to ask questions and have conversations to learn if people had a relationship with Jesus or had certain things to be praying about, I knew I would need an interpreter. All of them were occupied elsewhere. After praying for help and continuing to search, a lady (I think she was from the church hosting the clinic) said, "My daughter is only 14 and hasn't done a lot of interpreting, but she is willing to help." I accepted her help readily. She did a great job. It was such a blessing to be able to converse with the people and pray with them, which God made possible through the gentle, courageous teenager willing to step out of the boat and offer her skills. She helped me at various times during the rest of the week, her smile wide as she gained confidence. God shows again and again, as you step outside your own comfort and abilities, He provides for His people. Sometimes through you and sometimes in you.

## True Victory
*Lloyd DeFoor, Non-medical Servant*

I learned a long time ago that the focus of team leaders on trips should be the teams that are with us from the United States. We should pour our hearts and souls into them. Our worship times are so important. My goal for each trip is for every team member to have a face-to-face encounter with Jesus. We do not cut corners in our worship times! Also, another important focus should be on the translators. We will be in the country for a week or two. The translators are there permanently. When we started going on trips, the translators did not worship and meet with us. They would meet separately if they met at all. We invited the translators to start meeting with us, and everything changed. We no longer had an American team and a Nicaraguan team, or you name the country, we had a unified God's team. The bond between translators and the teams grew tremendously.

In El Salvador, our translators are students in the Christian school. They used to meet up with us at the clinic site. Several years ago when we were serving with Pastor Mauricio, I talked to him about the possibility of the students coming to our worship times at our hotel in the mornings. He thought it was a great idea, and they began to meet with us the next morning. What a difference their presence made as we sang and praised the Lord. We always have someone share a devotion and someone share a testimony. I also ask someone from the country in which we are serving to share also. It is important for our team to hear their stories. At the start we all think we are so different from the other, but slowly realize how very much alike we really are. We may look different, sound different and have different cultures, but we all have the same hopes and dreams and, most importantly, the same Lord and Savior.

On Wednesday night, a couple of the translators asked me if they could share Thursday morning, and I told them that would be wonderful. The young man shared first, and his presentation was incredible. Tears were on all of our faces as he told how the Lord was impacting his life and the lives of his family. And then it happened. This beautiful young lady, probably 16 or 17, started sharing. She shared her testimony about what a great God we served and about her relationship with Jesus. She talked about spending eternity with Jesus, but she also talked about the peace, comfort and power Holy Spirit gives us as He abides in each of us. She talked about how important it was to tell others about Him and how important our GHO mission trip was in sharing the gospel with the people in her community and country. She then shared these words that we all need to ponder. She said she wanted to live for Jesus, but if she had to, she would die for Him! How many of us can truly make that statement?

These two young people from El Salvador taught us an important lesson that day. What are we willing to give up in our service to the Lord and His children? What sacrifices do we make to advance the kingdom here in the U.S. and around the world? To add a little to the story, on Friday we had a picnic lunch provided by a member of the local church in a beautiful garden. All of the sudden I heard screaming of joy and crying taking place. I did not have a clue what had happened. One of the senior boys serving as a translator had accepted Jesus as His Savior. He was one of the leaders in their group from an influential family. This group of young people serving as our translators taught us another lesson. They had been praying with and for this young man for a long time. They had been sharing about this magnificent Savior we serve with him. To them, this was a time to rejoice and give God the glory for working in the life of this young man. Do we get as excited about the salvation of someone as we do a victory on the football, soccer or baseball field? This group of young people knew what true victory is, and that is when a brother or sister comes into a personal relationship with Jesus and he or she will spend eternity with us.

## Wherever We Are
*Celia Schoen, RN*

I was blessed to serve on a small mission trip to El Salvador. I always have a hard time reflecting and organizing my thoughts when I come back. While there, we stay so busy! Then, we come back and get busy again with the usual routines. Many have asked me, "So, how was your trip?" I always answer, "It was great," or "Amazing," but I have so much more to say!

I think many people put those who "go" on a pedestal, in a way. Like, somehow, they are "more Godly" or "super Christians." That bothers me. I am not some extraordinary person who's going out there to save the world. I'm just me. I do know and feel that I have been called to love and serve "the least of these." But aren't we all? Should we not also do this each day, regardless of location or vocation? Absolutely.

When we arrived in El Salvador, we were greeted by our amazing national partner team who patiently waited for all of our members to arrive and for all of our luggage to be searched. I am talking about two to three hours, just at the airport. These brothers and sisters, our gracious hosts, then tirelessly guided us daily to and from the clinic, to meals, to special outings to see more of the amazing country and experience its culture. We were exhausted! I can imagine how even more exhausted they felt. The planning, the early mornings and late nights, hearts poured out, living sacrifices. Absolutely beautiful portraits of servant leadership. What an example they set for sacrificial dedication in order to show love to those who needed it.

We attended their local church. Anyone could tell these brothers and sisters were Spirit-filled. Even when, at times, things were not being translated, we could feel the Spirit moving. These brothers and sisters are not just receivers of missionaries or charity. They are senders! They take the Great Commission very seriously. They are continually (long before we arrived, and long after we have gone) caring for the community we worked in for only a week. They are committed to sharing the gospel and bringing a quality, Christian education to an area with great need. An area stricken by violence, poverty and illness, with families with little to no spiritual leadership. At least 70 percent (or more) are single mothers struggling to provide for their children. In addition to their "Jerusalem," they also send missionaries out to "Judea, Samaria and the ends of the earth." Included in their efforts are the Middle East and the United States!

It's easy to be deceived sometimes. I think we sometimes forget that we are not the point. Our church, the "little 'c' church," is not the church. Christ's church spans across the world, and our local churches are a part of that. Revelation 7:9 talks about a great multitude, from every nation, tribe, tongue. The church is far bigger than we can imagine. It's easy to forget this as we sit through our "routine" church services. We start to get annoyed because the preacher isn't inspiring enough, or the music isn't to our liking, or there aren't enough activities, or there are too many activities...whatever, we pick it apart endlessly. But if we could just zoom out and realize that the body of Christ is way bigger than we can imagine, I'm convinced those complaints could not possibly hold any weight in our hearts.

Now, the clinic side of the mission trip isn't glamorous. Our small team of 10 saw around 1,000 patients in four and a half days of clinic. We had very basic medications, many that are readily available over the counter. Others, such as antibiotics, were also dispensed, though supplies of all were finite. One of the many things I noticed was the gratitude! By the end of the week, we were out of many of the medications we had brought. We had to turn some away with only vitamins and a prayer. But, even then, there was thankfulness. They accepted prayers and hugs and thanked us! For what? For our time, for caring, for showing love, for stepping out of our comfort zone to tell them they are loved and valued. What are some areas in our lives where we focus on the deficit, big or small, only to miss the blessing?

The need is great, both physically and spiritually. "Let's not become discouraged in doing good, for in due time we will reap, if we do not become weary. So then, while we have opportunity, let us do good to all people, and especially to those who are of the household of the faith" (Galatians 6:9-10, NASB).

I have been asked many times, why can't I just serve here, right where I am? Every day should be our mission. Some days, that's right here at home. Some days it's on a short-term mission trip. And some of us are called to long-term missions.

Why do I feel like I need to go to another country to serve God? The answer is because we are commanded to go. It isn't about the glamour of traveling to some exotic place, having an adventure or going sight-seeing. It's about loving our global family, those who are already a part of it, and reaching out to those who don't know Jesus yet. But may servant leadership, selfless love, care, compassion, kindness, sacrifice, gratitude, faithfulness, grace and obedience be wherever we are.

*Editor's Note: Celia is currently serving two years in the Middle East. She was inspired into long-term missions after this short-term experience.*

# ETHIOPIA
### 9.1450° N, 40.4897° E

## Trust God With Your Needs
*Anthony Sheplay, MD*

I have been going to Ethiopia with GHO for more than 12 years. Customs has always been a challenge, especially with medications. The rules and regulations constantly change as well as the level of scrutiny in customs. Our national partner would always obtain approval for the medications through the Ministry of Health as well as customs. Despite this, we always seemed to have delays. One particular year, the custom officials were particularly difficult.

We had the approvals and paperwork that were required by the government agencies. However, as we entered Ethiopia at the Addis Abba Airport, the officials told us the paperwork was insufficient. Furthermore, the rules had changed the week before! They confiscated about 75 percent of our medications. The only reason we still had 25 percent left is because several team members were let through ahead of the rest. We spent at least six hours at the airport trying to convince the officials to release our medications in light of the humanitarian nature of our trip. Despite showing our approval letters, request by local officials for our clinic and our GHO credentials, none of the eight officials would release our medications.

Our national partner suggested he and I remain behind in the capital to meet with high level government officials and get the medications released the next day. The team traveled to our destination, Meki, Ethiopia, led by our pharmacist. Along the way they were able to purchase a few medications, but as is usually the case in Ethiopia, it was difficult to find the medications we needed. For two days our national partner arranged meetings with various government officials. Each one seemed sympathetic and wanting to solve our problem, but in the end, no one wanted to take the responsibility to release the medications. Instead, we were referred to another official who was "very likely" to help us. We never did succeed in having the medications released. At this point, I felt our ability to conduct a useful medical clinic was significantly impaired.

Nevertheless, we decided to proceed with the clinic in Meki, understanding we would be limited and may need to close the clinic early. But, due to God's providence, we seemed to always have just the right medication for the needed problem. No patient left the clinic without the medication they needed! In addition, we had fewer cases than usual which required medications but instead could be treated by non-pharmacologic means.

On the way back to the capital, an orphanage requested we stop by for a half-day clinic. We had very limited medications at this point, and we almost declined the visit. The team, however, along with our national partner really wanted to help out at the orphanage. We were able to treat every child who needed it, and when the pharmacist filled the last prescription, he was out of medications! God had provided for our every need, even when we did not trust completely that He would come through for us and the people in Meki. We all learned an important lesson from that trip: trust God with your needs. Our team verse for the trip became Proverbs 3:5, "Trust in the Lord with all your heart, and do not lean on your own understanding. In all your ways acknowledge him, and he will make straight your paths" (ESV).

# THE GAMBIA
## 13.4432° N, 15.3101° W

## God Saves at His Good Pleasure
*Frank Imbarrato, MD*

It was the first GHO trip to the Gambia with a new national partner. The team was quite large for an African trip. The anticipation in
the local community was ramped up by national advertising through
television and radio. There was great expectation for free healthcare
by an American team coming to serve the community. We were well
received at the airport by dignitaries and the local press including
television.

The first day of clinic was pure chaos. Hundreds of people were
waiting for the team upon its arrival. There was no prior day organization or setup. The team was experienced and knew what to do and
how to get ready for the clinic. It was a matter of getting the crowd
under control so the clinic could begin with some semblance of order.
The locals who were giving out the registration papers didn't understand the process and procedure, and all the clinic papers were dis-
tributed within the first hour.

As team leader and with my assistants, we spent the initial hours
in the morning getting people organized and helping locals control
the crowd. We were troubleshooting the different areas of the clinic
and were walking around the clinic answering questions and helping
where we were needed. There were masses of people aimlessly walking around. People were being turned away once the papers were all
gone, and people were frantic knowing they were not going to see the
physician or dentist.

# GOD SIGHTINGS

There was a young gentleman who was so persistent in asking me for help and for a paper to see the doctor. No less than three times did he asked to be seen. I apologized to him that the papers were all handed out, but we could possibly see him tomorrow. The last time I apologized to him, he boldly said my apology was not accepted and that he needed help. His English was quite good. I took him aside and we discussed his issues. As we walked over to the side of the clinic toward the pharmacy, I noticed he was limping, and we talked about his hip and his pain. The hip pain was chronic and was not his main chief complaint. He explained that he had severe, painful hemorrhoids that were bleeding and he needed help. He was traveling the next day and could not return, and he felt unable to tolerate the pain.

He related to me that he had a master's degree in public health and was very interested in what we were doing in the clinic. He was Muslim, and I shared with him the reason we come to serve is to proclaim and show the love of Jesus through healthcare. I felt convicted in saying that when I had just turned him away three times. We were in a room by the pharmacy where the Bibles and tracts were being stored. After I examined him and treated him, we talked some more, and he expressed great interest in the gospel. He said he knew of Jesus and thought he knew who Jesus was. He had read parts of the Bible in the past and wanted to know more. I shared the gospel with him, and he accepted Jesus as his Lord and Savior. He eagerly accepted a Bible and accepted follow up information to get connected with local Christians.

He left the clinic thankful for the help he received and, even more so, joyful for his newfound life in Christ. The pain he had seemed better already, and he was even limping less. It was a humbling and joyful experience. God saves at His good pleasure for His purposes and for His glory. Not even hurried, distracted team leaders can stop His kingdom advance. It is to God's honor that the Holy Spirit can introduce Jesus to His chosen ones anywhere, anytime. Even through hemorrhoids.

# GHANA
## 7.9465° N, 1.0232° W

## Hope
### Diane Matsumoto, MD

It started as a simple Google search: medical missions July 2013. It was supposed to be a bonding trip with my daughter, a college essay and perhaps a treatment for emerging professional burnout. The email that followed my simple inquiry would change my life. "You are the physician we have been praying about." You have to be kidding, I thought. I suspected few healthcare mission team leaders would pray that the only other physician who would sign up for their trip to Africa would be a feisty suburban pediatrician with a fear of flying, no mission experience and no knowledge of tropical medicine.

Six months later I found myself one of only two doctors and one physician assistant in a tiny village in Ghana, West Africa (a country I had to look up to find on a map). In the first few days, I realized I had been transformed from a confident, competent physician to a student, treating diseases that had only been a paragraph in a textbook in my medical school training. Malaria, Schistosomiasis, malignant hypertension, worms, etc. Sitting shoulder to shoulder treating 80-year-olds, running every patient by the team leader, it had been a painful experience in humility.

Finally, on day four, it appeared my time had come. The triage team ushered in a young mother with 1-month-old twins. I was stunned as the woman laid down two profoundly malnourished twins. I watched as they had agonal breathing, knowing they were dying before my eyes. Their mom had no breast milk. I knew how to treat this. You call

911, rush them to the emergency room, insert lines and breathing tubes, send them to the ICU and carefully bring them back to life. This was Africa, however, with no IV fluids, no formula and no electricity.

In hindsight, what happened can only be God. God gave me only one thing: His grace among His people. In some sort of out-of-body experience, I found myself grabbing cut off water bottles and jumping in front of the crowd pleading for breast feeding moms to come to our help. On that small team, God had placed a NICU nurse. As women volunteered, we helped them pump their breast milk, the liquid gold we would use to resuscitate the babies. Over the next few hours, we would drip in drops of donated breast milk into their mouths. God would be the "IV pump." As I suspected, no one in the world could possibly know what rate to run in the life-giving fluid in a metabolic emergency with no labs or monitors. Slowly their breathing had stabilized.

The next few days would be a blur. The woman would return to clinic and we would strategize about how to get breast milk for her babies. In my heart, I believed I had bought her time, a chance to say goodbye to her children.

The last day would be the celebration ceremony which was presided over by the village priest. As we were preparing to leave, God placed it on my heart to go talk to the chief. Grabbing cut off water bottles and leftover syringes I had in my bag, I handed them to him. "I believe you are a great man. I believe God can help you care for these babies. I am giving you these to help these babies survive." Getting back on the bus I knew it was in God's hands, not mine. Their chances of meaningful survival were minimal, but I had done my best. Years later, I would come realize that I had crossed every social norm in Ghanaian culture.

One year later, I was back in the same West African country. A lot had changed. I had fallen back in love with medicine again. I had studied tropical medicine and adult medicine to prepare for the trip, and I no longer felt like a student. On the third day of clinic, a young woman approached me with her toddler twins. My translator smiled and told me, "These are your twins. God has brought them back to you so you could see and know He is there." God had showed up. The village chief had arranged for women to help feed the babies until they were old enough to take solids. Two years later I would be giving my testimony to hundreds of Ghanaians with two preschoolers at my legs.

You see, my God sighting is about hope. It is hope in a medical miracle and a second chance, using those who are broken and unfit for the job. Perhaps I was the doctor they had been praying for after all.

# GREECE
## 39.0742° N, 21.8243° E

## They Will Know Us By Our Love
*Jack Pike, PA*

I was in Athens, Greece with a GHO mission team to minister to Syrian refugees. This team was different from our usual mission team. Since we were serving Arabic speaking refugees in Greece, most of the church we were serving alongside did not speak Arabic either. So, our national partners helped arrange to fly in Palestinian Christians from Israel to serve as our interpreters. Many of these interpreters were young and had flown from Nazareth just to be part of our mission team. We also had several workers at the church who were actually a part of their sister church in Cyprus. Our international team consisted of members from the U.S., Cyprus, Greece and Israel! That alone was a real blessing to our team!

I had a young man assigned to me as an interpreter, and throughout our week serving together, we had many opportunities to talk and share about our lives and faith journey. This young man told me he had only been a Christian for about five months and had still not worked up the courage to tell his parents. He still lived at home and was reading his Bible, which made them curious. He related to me how he had been visited by Jesus in a dream that led him to salvation. This is not an uncommon way Jesus reaches the Muslim population.

Throughout the clinic week, several patients would come in the morning to our clinic and then wait around for the food distribution. The Cyprus members of our team were cleaning the clinic area daily and doing an organized food distribution early in the afternoons. One of the women who had come the first day of our clinic continued to come to the clinic each day. She would mostly sit in the small waiting room and just watch. She would watch the nurses at triage as they would interact with patients. She watched the reading eye glass clinic in the same room. She was quiet and just wanted to be there. She wasn't asking to be seen every day. Just watch.

Finally, our last day of clinic arrived. It always comes so quickly! She went up to one of our team's interpreters to speak with her. She wanted to share some of her observations. She told her she had watched the nurses working all week and how kind they were. She said they would smile at everyone! They would touch them gently on the shoulder or arm, help them and seemed to genuinely care about them. She seemed confused! She told the interpreter, "I have never seen that before! My people don't do that. Why are they helping us?" The interpreter told her "It's Jesus! We have Jesus in us." She went on to explain the gospel message to her. The interpreter had the idea to take her upstairs so one of the young interpreters could share his testimony with her.

It turns out, I had seen her husband several days earlier. I clearly remember his testimony because it was so tragic. Four of their children, all sons, who were killed in one day by a bomb. I cannot imagine her grief! She was up there to speak with the young, new believing interpreter. They talked for quite a while, and as the interpreter shared his testimony, it brought tears to his eyes. He poured his heart into sharing his experience with her. After he had finished, she asked her interpreter if he would help her pray to accept Jesus Christ as her Savior. It was a beautiful picture of living out the gospel message right before her eyes. You never know, in a busy mission clinic, who is watching! "By this everyone will know that you are my disciples, if you love one another" (John 13:35, NIV).

# GUATEMALA

## Give Us Ears to Hear
*Trish Burgess, MD*
*Director, Global Health Outreach*

I was serving as a physician in Guatemala. Near the end of our clinic week, I saw a young woman who presented complaining that her "ears are clogged." She went on to describe how they had been this way for months and were mildly painful, as well as causing her to have a hard time hearing. She had even been to an ENT who told her he had cleaned out one side a week or two before, but he only did one side and told her she needed to come back to have the other side done. She didn't have the money to go back.

I looked at her ears, and both sides were completely filled with hard, dry wax. So, I spent about 30 minutes trying to clean the wax out of her ears. It was difficult to remove because it was dried out and hard, so I would put in ear wax softening drops, wait a bit, then try to remove some. I removed as much as she could tolerate with what we call a cerumen (wax) spoon and then proceeded to flush her ears with warm water. I had help from a physician assistant student as well. After about a half hour, we had gotten out as much as possible, but they both still had some wax in them. Since it was near the end of our clinic week, I gave her my bottle of ear wax softener that should help the rest drain out as she continued to use it.

After all this, I asked her about her faith. She told me she believed in God but not in religion. I asked her if I could share with her about my God, Jesus. She readily agreed. I shared the gospel message with her using the Evangecube. She had tears in her eyes when I asked her if she had any questions. She explained that she believed in the message I shared with her. She said, "After you worked so hard to help me with my ears, I knew your God was the true God. I just knew!" She accepted Jesus Christ as her Savior with tears flowing down her face. It was a beautiful moment. God really can do amazing things with what seems like the little we have to offer in His name. It doesn't have to be big or dramatic for the Holy Spirit to use us to reach His people. There is no greater joy than being used as His instrument, as His hands and feet helping a hurting world.

## God's Plans Are Eternal
### Sheila Foxworthy, RN, and James Foxworthy, MD

We have our plans, our mission. Leading a general surgical team to Guatemala takes an enormous amount of planning and preparation, particularly with needed supplies. We have amassed not only the typical medications, but also anesthesia medications, disposable surgical drapes, sterile gloves in all sizes, suture material, prosthetic mesh, every conceivable item that might be required to perform a short-term surgical mission trip. Literally, an expert team has been assembled to perform the task before us.

We arrive the weekend before our surgeries are planned to begin to further screen our patients and make even more plans. This is a time of uniting with our national partner in the country. We rely on them to help pre-screen our patients as well as care for them and continue follow-up after our team leaves for home. In addition, the operating room is organized, we again screen patients who have been waiting all day or sometimes longer to be scheduled for a long-awaited procedure to alleviate physical suffering. It is our prayer that, in addition to physical healing, we can bring the hope of the gospel to them.

Monday comes, the boxes have all been checked and the schedule for the week is largely set. We meet in the morning, share devotions and begin our work. We are driven, one case at a time, to complete the task the Lord has set before us. We are succeeding to bring some hope to a small village in Guatemala, to bring some healing of the physical suffering of a few of its residents and some of the surrounding communities. Yes, we are faith based and we bring the love of Christ, but so often our attention is on our task at hand. That is a lot of what our life is like every day. We are not just on mission when we leave for another country, but our daily lives should be lived on mission. In the busyness of daily life, though, it can be easy to forget that!

On this particular mission trip, in the middle of the week, we were asked to evaluate a patient in a small clinic/emergency room. He had massive ascites secondary to end stage liver disease. He was not on our schedule of procedures, and, in fact, we had little to offer him from a medical perspective. This can often be the case, and it never gets any easier. As we explained to him his condition and our limited ability to help him, we all felt very inadequate. Stanley, our friend from Guatemala for many years and one of our translators, was with us and helping to interpret. Much of the conversation was in Spanish as he interpreted what we were trying to communicate to the patient. We noticed that Stanley and our patient were both in tears. Asking Stanley about this, he explained that he led this man to the Lord during that brief encounter. Our efforts for the temporary were laid low by God's plans for the eternal. Perhaps this one encounter was our reason for being in Guatemala that week. It is very humbling. To be a witness for the Lord using the very skills and knowledge He has given us is a beautiful experience, but perhaps even more beautiful is being in a front row seat to see God at work around the world! In His goodness and mercy, He lets us be involved or to join Him. It is also amazing to understand that He gives us that as a gift, not because He needs us. "Many are the plans in a person's heart, but it is the Lord's purpose that prevails" (Proverbs 19:21, NIV). It is an honor and a privilege to serve God through healthcare missions.

## He Began to Read
*Jim Byrkit, MD, and Jacque Byrkit*

When we were in Guatemala in March, we were working in one of the poorest barrios near the city dump. On the third day of our medical clinic, Jacque and I were in the pharmacy area when she discovered some prescription eyeglasses that one of the team members had brought. We have a station for reading glasses, because there is often so much need for them, but many cannot afford them. We typically do not give out distance or prescription glasses because it takes some expertise to size them correctly. We need to have an optometrist to be able to determine the appropriate size needed, or at least someone trained in missionary optometry.

Jacque asked me if I thought she should take them to the eyeglass area. I told her no, since we do not dispense them. Well, she did what any obedient wife would do...that is, a wife who is obedient to the Holy Spirit—she took them down to the eye station anyway. When she arrived, she found a teenage boy who had come with eager anticipation because he was unable to learn in school due to vision problems. He had tried on ALL of the various strengths of reading glasses we had available and was crestfallen because none of them allowed him to read. The moment Jacque arrived, he was feeling devastated and just preparing to leave. The team member gave him that pair of prescription glasses and instantly he began reading and reading and reading. Excitement and joy were all over his face. He left a happy boy, and we all witnessed a miracle.

If she had taken the glasses down there earlier or a couple of minutes later, or the team member had not thrown the glasses into her luggage as an afterthought, we would not have seen God give this boy a miracle. Who knows how his life will change with the ability to study and read? We often aren't allowed to see this far into God's stories, but we know it could change this boy's life.

These types of stories have occurred time and again on our mission trips. They have given us an insatiable addiction to continue to serve Him in missions. It is both exhilarating and humbling to see Him work through us by allowing us to be a tiny part of His great work.

# HAITI

18.9712° N, 72.2852° W

## Divine Healing
*Carolyn Grosvenor, MD*

This GHO trip to Haiti was almost cancelled because of the small size of our team: only 13 members. Usually there were more than 30 team members on the trips to Haiti, but, for some reason, GHO saw fit to send us anyway. Five years after the massive earthquake, displaced Haitians established a community in what once was a city dump. They cleared away the rubble and started building homes of their own. Many of them were still living in shacks since building a home often took years. They could only build one concrete block at a time as they earned money.

While in the clinic a woman brought her mother in to be seen. I called her "Mama." That's what I call all of the older Haitian women. Mama was on medication for diabetes and high blood pressure. (Mama actually brought her medications with her!) She came in wearing flip flops, hopping on one foot and dragging the other one as her daughter supported her. As soon as I saw her, I knew I didn't have anything in my bag to help her. She'd had a stroke and was paralyzed on the left side, both the arm and leg. Mama had had a stroke a week ago. Before I did anything else, I asked our physical therapists if we had a walker we could give her. We did, but the physical therapy assessment showed that a walker wouldn't help her. She had no grasp in the hand and no control over the leg. So, I took a history, did a brief exam and ordered some of her regular medications for her. The stroke was likely due to uncontrolled high blood pressure. She'd run out of her medications and was only recently able to get to the doctor to get more. She had the stroke after that doctor's appointment.

I then did a spiritual assessment and asked her if she knew Jesus. Her response didn't require a translator. She raised her good arm and started praising Him in Haitian Creole. I then told her I had nothing in my doctor bag that would help her walk again, but I would pray and ask the Lord to heal her. I reminded her that where two or three are gathered in His name He is present with them, and that what we ask for will be granted. I prayed that the Lord would heal Mama and enable her to walk not just for her benefit, but for His glory. I prayed that He would heal Mama so she would be able to dance before Him in the sanctuary and declare to an unbelieving world that Jesus is God! That He is alive! That He is faithful! And that He alone has the power to heal!

We had a "church service" there in my exam room. Then we said, "Amen," and it was time to help Mama "hop" back home. Mama stood up and lifted up her left foot and stepped over the extension cord! I was stunned. "Whoa, Mama!" Then she took another step, alternating steps. Then we started down the hallway and I called to our physical therapist. Can we have the walker now? As we walked down the hallway, we created quite a ruckus. When we got to the end of the hallway, we sat Mama down. We "just happened" to have a pair of sneakers that fit her, so I took off my socks and we put the sneakers on her and walked back the other way. The physical therapist gave her daughter some exercises to do to help Mama gain more strength and mobility. Then the physical therapists, along with a security guard, walked Mama down the hallway and out the back door which was closer to her home.

Afterward I asked myself, "Why was I so surprised when Mama stepped over the extension cord with her paralyzed leg?" While fervently praying I really believed that the Lord could heal Mama. I just didn't expect Him to do it right then. But Mama knew her Jesus and believed He could and would heal her right then and there.

That experience changed me forever. Now when I pray for someone's healing I really believe and expect the Lord to heal. And even if it doesn't happen immediately, I still believe for healing, until He tells me to stop. I know His grace is sufficient for every ailment. So why wasn't our small team of 13 cancelled? Because God had plans for Mama!

## Eyes to See
*David Maddy, DDS*

On a trip to Haiti with GHO, God spoke to me! I had practiced dentistry for 31 years in Florida. During this time, I came to the Lord because of my first mission trip that I joined after 16 years of doing dentistry. That trip changed my life, and after that I made yearly trips until I retired in 2012. I had been blessed to have visited many areas of the world and had taken my family, friends and church members with me. My daughter started going with me at age eight and went most every year until she moved out to go to college. We had a children's ministry component that supplemented our medical/dental care. As she aged, she became the leader of this ministry. She had been mentored and trained for such a task. Then one day she challenged me to start training the next generation of dental missionaries just like I had mentored her. Right to my heart she spoke.

Not only did I retire from my dental practice in 2012, I also joined as faculty at the University of Louisville School of Dentistry to fulfill my daughter's prophetic challenge. As I looked for my first dental student mission trip, I teamed up with GHO because our school had a local CMDA chapter. That is when I met Ron Brown, the GHO Associate Director, who is a mission team leader and my brother in Christ. We were going to Haiti!

It was a large team with physicians, dentists, medical students, dental students, pastors and lots of logistic or non-medical helpers. The group I will never forget were the two physical therapy students. I first met them when we were loading up the bus to make a 14-hour drive across the mountains to our work site. They were putting up several wheelchairs, lots of walkers and canes on the roof. There were so many I could not believe they got them to Haiti by plane. And I could not understand why or what they would be used for. Those students had a vision that was much greater than mine.

The clinic week went well. At the first night's debriefing, the physical therapy students told the group a story about a young girl. She was born with cerebral palsy and most everywhere she went she had to be carried by her father. They took out a walker, showed her how to use it and then God showed up. For the first time in her life on her own, the little girl started to step with the walker. In no time, she was running in circles, and all were praising God! At the second and third night debriefings, the physical therapy students told of more God sightings. I wanted to be in their area of the clinic to wait for God to appear, but I could not because I needed to be with the dental students. However, Ron was not going to miss the next God sighting.

The next day Ron came into the dental clinic all excited, and he wanted me to get my camera and come out into the courtyard. I grabbed my camera and came out fast. The two physical therapy students were standing behind a young man sitting in one of their wheelchairs. They were glowing with excitement. There was another young man standing next to his friend in the wheelchair. Ron and I watched as they pushed the young man and I asked them to stop so I could take a picture. As I was focusing my camera, my eyes were opened and I started to see what God was showing me. I said to Ron, "Look at the guy's knees, his shins and the top of his feet—callouses everywhere. Look at his calves, small and shriveled with no muscle." Haiti is a rough place, lots of gravel and rocks on the road. His calves were like that because he could not walk. The callouses were there because he got around his whole life by sitting on his knees and feet using the knuckles of his hands to drag along the ground in the rough gravel. Ron and I both started to tear up, and he said to me, "How come we have to come so far from home to see the mighty hand of God?"

You see, God had a plan for that wheelchair that was put on the roof of the bus. The one that I wondered why it was even brought. And there could not have been a better plan for that chair. One of His children in great need had suffered for years dragging himself along the gravel and was now redeemed. As Ron and I continued to watch with our emotions recovering, we were happy to see his friend was there to help him by pushing the wheelchair. But then our eyes were again opened, and we saw that his friend's arms were misshaped and could not be used. We teared up more.

Then God spoke to me and said, "You don't have to go so far to see my mighty hand, you just have to open your eyes and see."

## God Showed Up
*Mike O'Callaghan, DDS*

I have been privileged to serve on about 35 GHO mission trips thus far. I have seen God work in numerous different ways. As I prayerfully considered which of the many stories of God at work through GHO to share, I was surprised that the Lord led me to share this one. It is not what I personally think of as a traditional, exciting short-term mission trip story. Nonetheless, it was one of the most significant experiences in my life to date. Additionally, I believe God often works powerfully in our own lives as we step out to serve others in His name.

In the summer of 2005, our middle son Dan asked me if we could go on a short-term healthcare mission trip together the following summer. Though I hadn't served on a mission trip thus far, I liked the idea, and we began planning.

I had heard several stories from patients about how they got to "pull teeth" on short-term mission trips, which they invariably described as "awesome." But as a practicing dentist, I did not think that having untrained people remove teeth represented "golden rule" healthcare. So, in searching for a suitable organization to work with, I thought of CMDA. I checked and was pleased to learn they had a short-term mission ministry called GHO.

As a member of CMDA, I figured GHO would not be a trip full of "yahoos" who viewed a short-term mission trip as an opportunity for unlicensed participants to play dentist for a day by doing surgery on vulnerable patients. The only GHO trip that was available and fit in our schedule was to Cap-Haitien, Haiti.

So, the next August, Dan and I arrived in Haiti with luggage packed full of dental instruments, disposable supplies and anything else I could think of. The pre-trip information regarding our dental clinic situation was sparse. We would get there and figure things out to the best of our abilities.

Monday was our first clinic day. Our GHO dental team consisted of me (a novice), Jim (a dentist who had served with GHO before), Jared and Lisa (two fourth year dental students), my son and Jim's two daughters, as well as three local volunteer translators. I was assigned to work in a folding metal "dental chair" in a dirty back room without any windows. There were no x-rays. I had neither a dental "drill" or suction. It was oppressively hot and humid.

My first patient was brought back by a translator wearing a GHO shirt. His name was Ronald. He was energetic and had an obvious, passionate love for the Lord. But Ronald had what might generously be defined as a poor understanding of English. And I knew absolutely no Creole.

I had never worked in this kind of primitive environment. In my pre-trip musings, I never considered such dire operating conditions. My son was my dental assistant, which was a totally new experience for him also.

After examining my first patient, I decided the most urgent need was to have her six upper front infected teeth removed. After a lengthy translation effort, which included using both words and impromptu sign language, I proceeded to treat the patient. After successfully removing the six offending teeth, I placed gauze in her mouth and got her to bite down on the gauze.

Next came the challenge of conveying the necessary post-operative instructions. As Ronald and I were laboring in this task, my son Dan visited the front of the clinic area where Dr. Jim was working. Dan came back and promptly reported, "Dad, Dr. Jim is sharing the gospel with his patients. You didn't do that!"

I was so overwhelmed trying to provide dentistry in this new setting that I totally forgot about sharing the gospel! I wanted to immediately right this wrong. I asked Ronald to ask the patient if she knew Jesus as her Lord and Savior. Ronald understood these words and began to fervently communicate with the patient. The patient tried to respond, but her mouth was filled with now blood-soaked gauze. It was a mess! That was how it went with my first GHO patient.

Toward the end of the second clinic day, an elderly man with significant skeletal deformities presented for removal of a severely infected and decayed tooth. He was unable to walk, and others assisted him into our clinic. After an examination, we tried our best to explain the complexity of his situation. With his seeming consent, I secured Lisa, a fourth year dental student, to be my assistant as more complex surgery was required. After an hour of struggling with dense bone and atypically bulbous roots, the tooth was finally removed. Upon discharging the patient, I felt terrible. I knew he would have significant post-operative pain and I was not confident we were able to adequately communicate with him. We had no ice to give him. He had no phone number that I could call to check on him later. It was frustrating providing care with so many limitations.

That night I woke up about 1:30 a.m. The other guys in my room were all sleeping soundly, yet I lay in bed wide awake. My soul was troubled, and I was not exactly sure why. I began to think and pray about the events of the last few days.

Somehow my attention was focused on that older man whose extraction was especially difficult. As I lay there, God began to work in my heart. I am not sure how to convey what happened. Maybe the best I can do is to say that God showed up.

In the past, sometimes I would pray asking God to show me how He sees me, asking that His Holy Spirit might search my heart and reveal ways that I displeased Him, especially where I was accustomed to my own sin. That sounds quite spiritual, doesn't it? I thought so too.

On that night, God did just that. He showed me that the primary reason I was upset about the care I rendered to that older, infirm patient was not because I was compassionate and loving. No, the primary reason I felt so troubled was not due to my loving empathy for this man with great trials, but because I was not able to perform the technically skilled dentistry that made me feel good about myself and that might impress Lisa, the dental student.

As that realization came to me, I knew it was true. What an arrogant, unloving, selfish, egotistical perspective! I lay in bed for about two hours, quietly weeping in the presence of God, as He shined the light of His Holy Spirit into the dark recesses of my heart.

Sure, I had a Christian veneer: a leader in my home church, Bible teacher to adults and an abstainer of smoking and alcohol. Yet, by His grace, God surgically exposed these ungodly remnants of my sinful nature.

God disciplines those He loves as His children. God does not bring condemnation for those in Christ, but conviction and repentance which empowers us to better follow Him and lead the new life in Christ He bought for us with His blood. Being broken by God is one of His choicest gifts.

When I woke the next morning, I felt like a new man or at least a man with a new perspective on life and ministry. The love of God poured through me to minister the compassion and love of Christ to each patient who entered our humble clinic. That changed everything.

That was 14 years ago now. Today, I long for heaven when the desire to sin will be removed after our glorification. Yet, as long as we live in the flesh, we must continue to fight the battle to yield to the indwelling Holy Spirit as opposed to yielding to the desires of our sinful human nature. I still fight that battle. Every day. But I am forever thankful for how the Lord used that first GHO trip to humble and redirect my wavering heart in a powerful way.

## Prayers in the Middle of Nowhere
*Carolyn Grosvenor, MD*

On my first trip to Haiti we served in Mirebalais, which is northeast of Port-au-Prince. Upon exiting the airport, the sights and sounds were rather distressing. Four years after the earthquake and Haiti was still in poor shape. Some areas were nothing more than a pile of rubble, and I gather that car maintenance is not a priority in Haiti. On the way north to Mirebalais one of our vans broke down, and we were stranded in the dark for a couple of hours while our Haitian partners drove back into town to get a part.

After serving in Mirebalais, we again had car trouble on the way back down off of the mountain. This time it was the van I rode in. The driver felt that something was wrong, so he pulled over on the side of the road. He and the driver of the other van, as well as several other men, checked the van and could find nothing wrong with it. So, we took off again only to pull over less than 10 minutes later. This time they found the problem and dispatched a car to go into town for the part.

We were on a highway and in the middle of nowhere, but when we pulled over the second time, we were right in front of a family's home. We got out of our vans and visited with the family. They lived in a shack and were slowly building a new home block by block. They welcomed us to tour their current home as well as the one under construction.

Our partner pastor approached me with a request from the home-owner's wife. Her husband, Joseph, was sick in bed, and she asked if I could examine him. He'd been to the doctor and was told he needed a chest x-ray, but they had no way to get to the hospital, let alone pay for an x-ray. So, I examined him in his bed. Based on what he told me, I suspected he had tuberculosis. I told the couple that I didn't have anything in my bag that would help him, but I knew someone who could.

After taking a spiritual history and learning they both believed in Jesus for salvation, I offered to pray for them. I recited what the apostle Peter said when faced with a beggar in need: "Silver and gold I do not have; but what I do have I give to you; Jesus!" (Acts 3:6, paraphrase).

I prayed for peace, for joy, for comfort and for supernatural healing. I reassured the couple that the Lord God, El Roi, sees them. That He has not forgotten them. That He is well acquainted with their situation and has a plan in place for their unique situation. That He will sustain them through this difficult time. By the time I finished praying I knew the Lord was present in that prayer meeting, and I could see their spirits had been lifted. As we said our goodbyes, I realized that, in His providence, the Lord caused our van to break down outside Joseph's home so I could give him and his wife a message of hope and encourage them to hold onto their faith.

When we stopped the first time, we weren't at our destination yet. That would explain why several men who "knew stuff" about cars could not find the problem. So, we drove a little further, and when the van finally broke down, I was right outside Joseph's sick room!

The Lord spoke to me. I was sent to Haiti for Joseph! He looked down from heaven and said, "I need to send someone to go encourage him to 'hold on to his faith.'" This was my first trip to Haiti; a trip that I didn't even want to go on, but the Lord pushed me into going! Then the van breaks down right outside Joseph's sick bed. The Lord had plans for me and Joseph. This was a divinely appointed encounter!

I don't want to spiritualize everything that happens on the mission field, but I can recall several trips where a specific team member was the only one able to minister to a specific person. The Lord goes out of His way to meet the needs of those who cry out to Him. What I have in my doctor's bag isn't what they really need. What they need is what the woman with the issue of blood needed, a touch from Jesus!

I don't know if Joseph was healed physically, but I do know his spirit was revived, and he was healed spiritually by a touch from Jesus.

# HONDURAS
## 15.2000° N, 86.2419° W

## Big and Little Things
*Kevin Smallwood, PA*

I have served on many GHO and other mission opportunities over the last several years, and we don't always get the chance to go out into the community to do home visits with those who are homebound and unable to get to the clinic. I was serving in Honduras and had the opportunity to go on a home visit.

Two other team members and I, along with our host missionary, went to visit Raphael and Lourdes. Raphael was 65 years old and the father of Lourdes, who was then 32 years old. Raphael was working in his wood shop when we arrived. He makes wood art for a living. The art he sells provides money so he can buy the medicines needed for Lourdes. You see, Raphael is the caregiver for Lourdes. Lourdes developed Polio at age seven, and the resultant disability rendered her unable to work. Raphael's wife died 23 years ago, leaving him alone to care for and provide for his daughter. It has been just the two of them since that time. Raphael works tirelessly to provide for Lourdes.

We were visiting to care for Lourdes. She was in reasonably good health. She had the typical ailments we had seen that week, mainly seasonal allergies, muscle pain and acid reflux. She also had hypertension that was diagnosed a year ago. She had taken her last pill for her blood pressure that morning. Thankfully, I had brought the right medicines for her with me! We were able to provide her with the medicine she needed to help with her ailments. It was no accident

God put this family into our path, nor was it an accident He allowed us to have the medicines to give to her.

We then asked Raphael if he had any needs. He mainly had musculoskeletal pain, and we were able to provide medicine to help with symptomatic relief. We then asked if they were Christians. Interestingly enough, Raphael told us he used to be a Catholic priest. He said he believes in God, but he does not attend a church. We asked if we could pray for them, and we did. They were so appreciative and thanked us for coming to see them.

This home visit and service opportunity was by far my favorite part of this mission trip. I thank God for this opportunity! I am thankful He allowed us to serve them through healthcare and the opportunity to pray for them specific to their needs. It is such a gift to let people know Jesus loves them just as they are and they are not lost or forgotten by God. I continue to pray that Raphael and Lourdes would be able to connect with a church. He cares for us in the big things and the little things of our lives. He demonstrated this in and through us on this home visit, also known as a divine appointment.

## Buenisimo
**Ron Brown**
**Associate Director, GHO**

"Malísimo" who became "Buenisimo," was a member of The 18 Gang in Villa Franca, on a tall mountain overlooking Tegucigalpa, Honduras.

We were serving in Honduras alongside Pastor Armando Meza, who had a youth ministry aimed at redeeming the gang members by introducing them to sports and getting them to join a soccer team, providing uniforms and soccer balls and, most importantly, introducing them to Jesus.

When we were setting up the GHO clinic in a public school that had been offered to us for the week, Pastor Armando came to me and said the gang leader of The 18 Gang for Villa Franca wanted to talk to me. I was expecting some menacing tattooed big thug, but as I entered the empty classroom, there was a 17-year-old teen with no shirt on, no tattoos and a very young appearing face and demeanor. He told me he had come to welcome our GHO team and they would be protecting us this week while we ran our GHO medical clinic in their Villa Franca. I never imagined being somewhat comforted at being told by a gang member that they would protect our team and clinic setting. Oh my, the anomalies of following the Lord.

Later I met the second-in-command of the Villa Franca 18 Gang. He was an older teen and used crutches to get around, as he had a birth defect that greatly affected him. I soon learned as we both got into the back of Armando's pick up truck that he used his crutches like a pole vault and was up and in much faster than I could climb in. I also imagined he had used them as a weapon when needed. I asked him his name and he said, "They call me Malísimo," which I knew meant the "very bad one."

We reconnected later that week one evening as we set up our big screen in the middle of two crossing streets to show the Jesus film. The gang members had invited more of their gang and their girlfriends to come "see the show." For some reason as we were watching the Jesus film, I whispered to Malísimo, "One day your name will change to Buenisimo when Jesus comes into your life."

Armando was getting them organized to form a soccer team, and he had brought them new uniforms and a new soccer ball. So, by the end of the week, we had engaged with them multiple times and finally said our goodbyes as we thanked them for protecting us and becoming our friends.

A few years later I was with another GHO team in another part of Honduras and I got a call from Pastor Armando, who had heard we were in country and wanted to know when we were departing. Our departure was the next day, and he told me he would meet me at the airport to greet me. When we pulled into the airport parking lot, there was Armando awaiting us, but so was this young man with crutches. This young man was literally beaming with a smile and a peace on his face that was amazing. The first thing out of his mouth was, "My name is not Malísimo anymore. They now call me Buenisimo, just like you said." He told me he had accepted Christ into his heart, as he pulled out his pocket Gideon New Testament and began reciting verses he was memorizing. Armando was discipling him to be a world changer, starting with his own 18 Gang.

## Dios te Ama
*Andy Lamb, MD*

"Sh-h-h ninito, no llores. Dios te ama. Sh-h-h little one, don't cry. God loves you." Over and over, I whispered these words to the frail, emaciated little Honduran boy as I gently stroked his thin, black hair. I didn't know his name or even his age, though I estimated him to be around a year and a half old. So frail, so sad, so frightened. My heart ached to comfort him.

I first met him an hour before. I was on a healthcare mission trip to the tiny town of La Esperanza in the mountains west of Tegucigalpa in Honduras. I was there as an internal medicine specialist with a team of others to provide basic medical care in an underserved region of Honduras. This was my fourth medical mission trip to Central America. The mission trips were a catharsis for my soul, cleansing me of the built-up frustrations and pressures from years in clinical medicine. Not even 50 years old, I was beginning to burn out, and more and more I wondered if I had made a mistake going into medicine. My heart was hardening, and my passion for healthcare and compassion for people was slowly eroding. These mission trips enabled me to experience medicine in its purest form, unencumbered by paperwork, managed care and a litigious society. I felt joy again in ministering to the beautiful people of Honduras. Little did I know that God, instead, would use a tiny malnourished child to minister to me. La Esperanza, which means hope in Spanish, would restore hope in me.

As I was seeing patients each day, several women on the team saw the need for the children to be bathed, deloused and dressed in clean clothes. They scoured the small town's stores and bought all the children's clothes and shoes they could find. An area was set up for bathing using large trashcans. Each child was washed, had his or her hair deloused and was given new clothes and shoes. The laughter and delight of the children reverberated throughout the clinic site. The word spread and more children came! As I witnessed this, I too wanted to be a part of this special ministry. I decided to take a half-day from seeing patients and instead spent the time helping wherever I could with the children.

He was first that day. He cried and cried ever so weakly, his dark eyes brimming with tears. His thin arms and legs covered with dirt, too weak to really resist the help we offered. As carefully as I could I cleaned him. He left dressed in fresh, new clothes and shoes. He was no longer crying, but not smiling either. An hour later he was back, his new clothes and shoes completely soiled and a feeble cry again on this thin, trembling lips. As he stood weeping, I carefully removed his clothes and shoes. I laid him down in the sun-drenched walkway and began cleaning him again. Thoughts of my own boys, now nearly grown, came to mind. I was overwhelmed with a need to show this little one the love and caring that was missing in his life; a life of poverty compounded by physical and emotional neglect. His crying continued, barely audible at times. He laid lifeless, hardly moving, head turned to the side where he continued to stare as if looking for someone. Suddenly, memories of rocking my own boys as infants came flooding into my mind. I began to whisper a soft, soothing "sh-h-h-h" in his ear, just as I had done with my sons, telling him again and again, "No llores, ninito, no llores. Dios te ama." His soft sobs eased, and he looked at me with his moist ebony eyes. He calmly lay there as I finished cleaning him, all the while continuing to whisper to him as lovingly as I could. Once he was dressed, he was taken away, to where I do not know.

In my brief encounter with this Honduran boy, I was reminded again of why I went into healthcare—to serve others. The years of demanding work, long nights on call, administrative headaches and managed care had slowly hardened my heart. God used this little one to begin a softening, one which continues today. And I am deeply grateful to serve in His name.

## God's Time
*Don Thompson, MD*
*Director Emeritus, Global Health Outreach*

The night nurse at the mission hospital in Guaimaca, Honduras walked with purpose through the jumbled medical instrument and supply room. She did not notice me on her way to the dormitories out back. I called out to her in Spanish just before she disappeared. "May I help you with something?" She quickly replied, "I'm looking for Dr. Nancy. We just had a lady come in who is 39 weeks pregnant, has a bad headache and a blood pressure of 190/120, and has protein in her urine." I trotted to keep up with her and told her that I would get Dr. Nancy. "How old is she? Has she had eclampsia before?" She replied, "She is 38 years old. She had a problem with a previous childbirth." Tick-tock, tick-tock....

Timing is everything. Seconds can count. It has been said, "God is rarely early, but He is never late." It was 9:45 p.m. on Monday evening. Our GHO team had arrived Sunday at the hospital being operated by Baptist Medical Dental Mission International (BMDMI) to provide general and gynecological surgery support, as the hospital was expanded to include two operating rooms and laparoscopic surgery. Monday was a frustrating day for the surgical team as they located the necessary surgical instruments and supplies and hoped that the light sources worked for the scopes. Instruments had to be sterilized at the last minute, as few surgical procedures had ever been done at this hospital. There was no laboratory and no blood bank. Yet. The surgical team had turned in at 9:30 p.m. after an exhausting day and a late dinner.

I went to the pink dormitory door where all the women were staying. I raised a quick prayer as I knocked. "God, please give these ladies energy and focus, and protect mom and baby." I pushed open the door and said, "Nancy, there is a 38-year-old at 39 weeks with headache, BP of 190/120 and proteinuria in the examination room." Nancy did not hesitate. She jumped out of bed, and she directed the operating room team on her way to the door. "Get set up for an emergency C-section in 15 minutes." No one hesitated as Joy, the circulating/charge nurse, and Jaimeson, the scrub nurse, tumbled out of bed, and I stuck my head through the blue dormitory door to awaken Shaun and Rodney, the anesthesia team.

Nancy did a rapid assessment of the mom. "She has hyperreflexia, decreased urine output and pitting edema to her mid-calves. I think she might be in DIC (disseminated intravascular coagulation). We have to deliver this baby now!" Tick-tock, tick-tock....

The hospital had no laboratory. Well, there was a room that had a sign that said "Laboratory," but there was no equipment and no supplies. There was no blood. No centrifuge. No serology. No ability to type and crossmatch blood. Nancy repeated, "Don, we have to deliver this baby!"

I woke up Dwight, the President of BMDMI, who happened to be visiting for a few days. He woke up the Honduran medical director, as she was in charge of the hospital and everything that took place there. We explained the risks of eclampsia to mom and baby, and the risks of doing an emergency C-section with no lab and no blood. We had anesthesia and oxygen. But we did not have time. The Honduran medical director thought about it for just a moment before she said, "Do it. I'll take responsibility for it. We have to try to save the mother and the baby."

By now, mom was in the operating room fully draped with a foley in place. Nancy said, "Don, you're the pediatrician. You are going to get a sleepy baby. We do not have blood, and we do not know if she can clot. I have to go slow. We cannot do coagulation tests." Shaun drew some blood into a red-top clot tube and taped it to the wall of the operating room as he started a timer. "It's supposed to clot within three minutes if there are no coagulopathies." Tick-tock, tick-tock....

I turned on the overhead lamps on the baby warmer and checked the batteries in the laryngoscope. I turned on the oxygen tank and connected the oxygen to the Ambu bag. Shaun said, "The blood clotted at three minutes exactly." Never early....

Jaimeson said, "Ready." Joy said, "Ready." Nancy looked at Shaun and Rodney and nodded. Shaun turned on the anesthesia gas and quickly pushed two syringes of medication into the IV. Rodney started the clock and reached for the laryngoscope and the endotracheal tube. "Go," he said as he cleanly passed the tube into the trachea.

Nancy made a midline skin incision and carefully dissected through fascia and muscle to the peritoneum. She identified and isolated the bladder and reached the uterus. She gingerly made a low transverse incision, carefully avoiding blood vessels. She reached the baby and carefully lifted baby through the uterine incision. She quickly clamped and cut the umbilical cord, wrapped baby in a blue towel that matched her skin color and passed her to me. I dried and stimulated baby for a few seconds and checked her heart rate. 70, but no respiratory effort. Floppy and no response to stimulation. One-minute Apgar: One.

The operating room was silent. I bagged her with a tiny mask on the Ambu bag as Joy continued to dry her and stimulate her. Heart rate up to 80. Several minutes later she started to pink up centrally. Heart rate 100. She started to grimace at five minutes. Five-minute Apgar: Five. Tick-tock, tick-tock.... At seven minutes Joy gave her with IM vitamin K in her right thigh, and she let out a holler. The room erupted in applause! Seven minutes of the most intense praying ever! Ten-minute Apgar: Eight.

God was not late. He was right on time. In the fullness of time, God sent forth His Son....

## God's Will Be Done
*Douglas B. Huene, MD*

During the orthopedic Honduras mission trips, we see clinic patients mostly on Saturday at two to three hospitals, then we operate doing total hip and knee replacements, hands, sports surgeries and sometimes spine surgery Monday through Thursday, packing up and doing a final inventory of our equipment on Friday to leave on Saturday. The clinics tend to be extremely busy with more people than we would ever be able to see. It is heartbreaking to send patients away, but it is also exhausting to see 150 patients who almost all are candidates for surgery. I am part of the total joint team and realize we will only be able to perform at most six knee replacements and four hip replacements during the week at one hospital. There have been many patients who I have told that we are unable to do their joint replacement, but they will have a greater chance when we return in six months, and the most common response I get is, "That's okay, thank you for coming and taking care of us and thank you for what you are doing for the Honduran people."

On one of the trips, the team had been working extremely hard in clinic and were exhausted. We were only to be at the hospital for a half day and tried to leave to get lunch at 11:30 a.m. before heading to the next hospital, but we found ourselves in clinic at 1 p.m. with many more patients to see. We had already selected our four patients and two alternates to do total knees on, plus we had 45 patients on the "waiting list" (meaning they would take the place of one of the six if they cancelled). While that sounds terrible to our American ears, the important thing I have learned in Honduras is that the main thing we can give the Honduran people is hope. Just by being there and seeing our smiling faces (despite exhaustion), we provide hope to them. We give priority to those who have come to the clinic numerous times and have had some patients come time after time every six months for seven or eight times before being selected. At 1:30 p.m., I was asked to see one more patient, José, who had never been seen before, but his wife was begging for her husband to be seen. I wondered, "Why would I do that? I'm already beyond overwhelmed with patients," but I figured we could "get him on the books" for another trip. This leads me to God sighting number one: my intake person's compassion for seeing this patient's needs beyond the mass of people who were still hoping to be seen.

I saw José, who had x-rays with some arthritis but was very immobile due to pain. He had some mild swelling in the knee and good motion. I had seen patients that were much, much worse already in clinic, and he was number 46 alternate on the list. There was no way he could get his knee done. I offered an injection to him but told him that if he took the injection to help with the pain, there is no way we would do his knee until possibly six months later when we returned. His wife asked if there was any chance of doing his knee and I told her "miniscule." She said if there is any chance at all of him being done, she would like to take it. (This is God sighting number two, which will become apparent later.)

The week went along, and the teams worked hard. The prayer team that travels through the hospital every day had their usual multiple God sightings and shared those with the group every evening. The operating room teams had their God sightings as well, which always encourages all the team members. As we came to the end of the week, we were running out of knee implants and only had large implants left. Being over-zealous doctors, we hoped to do an additional patient on Friday as one of the hospitals could not give us a room on one of the earlier days. We went through the 45 patients who were all too small, but the 46th patient, José, was the right size. We called the patient, who was ecstatic and gave credit to God for giving him this opportunity to have surgery (God sighting number three).

As José and his wife were in the pre-op area getting ready for surgery, the tests came back that his kidney function was impaired. We considered cancelling José's case for multiple reasons: the poor kidney function, we were tired, we wanted to get back to the hotel and pack equipment and it had been a long week. Just then the Honduran kidney doctor came by and felt he would be okay for surgery (God sighting number four). We decided to proceed.

We prayed before starting surgery, as we do before every patient, and asked God for wisdom and success. As we opened José's knee to do a knee replacement, pus drained out of the knee. José had a low-grade infection in his knee for much of the past year. Needless to say, we did not do a knee replacement, but if all the other things had not happened, José would still have a knee infection or, more likely, would have become septic and died. We washed out his knee joint aggressively and placed him on antibiotics. While I would love to tell you that José was pain-free and lived happily ever after, that would not be true. He did get resolution of his infection, however, and was able to return to walking, whereas before he was on crutches or a wheelchair. He is not a candidate for a knee replacement in the future, but the surgery probably saved his life and allowed him to return to walking. Maybe that is God sighting number five, that God works through every member of the team to accomplish His will. God allowed us to be His hands in the care of José and his wife.

## Life Changing Conversations
*Bill Sasser, DDS*

I have found that the Lord will often use a conversation with another in a powerful way without us even being aware of what He is doing at the time. This has likely occurred to me on many occasions when I wasn't even aware. However, there are three instances where God used one-on-one interaction on a GHO mission trip to bring big changes in the life of another.

The first occurred many years ago in Honduras when I had a teenage high school student assigned to the dental clinic as a helper. She was on the trip accompanied by her father who was a physician. I didn't realize it at the time, but many years later I received an email from her stating she had decided to make dentistry a career after having first felt God's call during that trip. A few years later I heard from her again that she had graduated and was in a general practice residency program continuing her education. One of her co-residents was a young dentist who had been a part of our student ministry. They were excited to know about their mutual connection with Dr. Bill and foreign missions.

The next was a lady who I met as a seatmate on a long flight. This was a divine appointment. Our conversation took the usual direction of asking about our lives and work. I, of course, told her about my involvement with international mission service, and the next thing I knew she had registered to come along on a GHO mission trip. She has subsequently been on a number of trips in a support role doing a great job, especially loving on older people and children. We have developed a deep friendship with her entire family.

The last of many such appointments was a lovely lady who came on a GHO mission trip many years ago, not being fully aware of how God might use her, but with an open heart. During the week we had a number of conversations about taking steps in faith and a willingness to be available as one of the most important ingredients in a life of surrender to the Lord. Subsequently, this lady quit her job so she would be able to go where the Lord might send her, trusting Him all the way. She went to seminary, has served on many GHO mission trips to the most challenging locations, has supported our dental student ministry and even spent time on a Mercy Ship.

You never know when a simple conversation can change the trajectory of your life! God seems to arrange many such divine appointments. I look forward to many more on my calendar.

## The Locked Door
*Mark Moores, MD*

I was serving as a family physician in Honduras but was one of the two designated pediatricians for this mission trip. A lot of people from the national church we were partnering with were helping. We had a lady guarding the door to our room or "office" for the week. She is basically the one who controls the flow into our room and allows patients to enter only when the doctor is finished with their patient and ready for the next patient. This is a key role as the clinics can get extremely busy with hundreds of patients who sometimes get impatient while they wait.

This servant from the national team was quiet and shy with us. She served well in her role, though, and things in our part of the clinic were running smoothly. We discovered over the course of our week that she was the wife of one of the local pastors, and she was volunteering her time to help us. So many pitch in and help not expecting anything in return, but simply wanting to help and be a part of our mission team.

The third day we arrived at clinic that morning as usual. When we got to our room, there was a large padlock on the door locking it. We were not able to get into our room. We were working at a school and so they got the school superintendent to try and unlock it for us. He had a huge ring of about 30 keys and began trying every single one of them. They did not know this padlock and were not sure where it had come from or who might have the keys to open it.

We typically do not stay right in the village where we are serving and were about 30 minutes away from the closest store where we may be able to buy some bolt cutters. We were discussing options of how we may get the lock open as more and more keys were being tried. That lock was not budging! Every key had been tried, the lock pulled on and tugged with no success.

After they had tried all his keys and were making a plan to go for the bolt cutters, the lady who guarded our door and controlled the patient flow asked if she could try. She touched the lock to try and open it and it suddenly fell open. Not with a key but simply by her soft, gently touch of the lock. Our jaws dropped! I actually felt a rush of fear! "Whoa!" was the only thing I could say. The Holy Spirit opened that lock! We all stood amazed at the miracle we had just witnessed! God works in ways that we can forget are amazing! Even in the small things. Why we had this delay I don't know, but I trust God had His reasons. His plan. We plan and prepare, but He makes our way!

## No Shows
### *Phillip L. Aday, DDS*

In a dental practice, missed appointments or "no shows" are a fact of life. No one likes them! They are a drag on production and a big waste of precious time. Such was, and often still is, my mindset in running my private dental practice. Taking that attitude with you on a GHO mission trip offering dental procedures can cause an internal struggle.

I was leading a GHO team to Santa Rita de Copan, Honduras with a large dental component of five dentists and a nice complement of medical professionals. We were set up in a local school, and, as usual, there were hundreds of people from the surrounding area lining up each day wanting to be seen by our healthcare professionals.

On the second day of clinic, Ricardo (our national partner) came to me letting me know there was a Cuban doctor in town who wanted to come and be seen by our dentists. Historically, over the last several decades Cuba has "exported" doctors to Central America. This has been a way of showing off the success of their medical system in an effort to increase the influence of Cuban socialism.

My initial inclination to Ricardo's request was to reject this Cuban doctor's request. My opinion was that the GHO team was here to treat patients who could not afford to see a local medical physician or dentist. However, I agreed to see this Cuban doctor by shortening my lunch break. This would allow our dental team to still have full availability to see the large number of local residents who truly could not afford to see a local dentist. I agreed to see this Cuban doctor the following day during my lunch hour. So, he was given an appointment.

The next day I saw patients during the morning and took a quick break at noon to eat lunch and began waiting in our dental area for my scheduled patient. The lunch hour came and went with the Cuban doctor being a no show. Did I mention that I dislike no shows? So, I thought, "That's it! I gave up part of my lunch hour and this guy didn't show up. That's it."

I spent the afternoon treating patients who had shown up early that morning and stood patiently in line waiting for their turn to be seen by our clinicians. That afternoon was a seemingly endless flow of dental patients. However, since we had a very robust dental team, by about 4:30 p.m. I was finishing the last patient we had promised to treat. Normally the dental area is second only to pharmacy as the last ones to complete the day's patients. This day, however, we were finishing a little early and I was looking forward to checking on the other treatment areas to assess how the day had gone.

At 4:35 p.m. Dr. Julio, the Cuban doctor, showed up holding a cake as an apology for missing his lunchtime appointment. Have I mentioned that I dislike no shows? So, just as I thought I was through seeing patients for the day, Dr. Julio showed up. My initial response was to tell this Cuban doctor who could afford to see a local dentist and who had "no showed" me that he was out of luck because he had missed his appointment. Thankfully, I listened to the Holy Spirit, who if we allow Him leads us in the way of righteousness, and agreed to change my plans of checking on the rest of the team at the end of the day.

As it turned out, Julio needed only a small anterior restoration and a cleaning. I was able to easily complete his needed treatment and be done before the pharmacy was finished dispensing prescriptions for the patients we had seen that day.

After I completed his dental care, I felt the Holy Spirit leading me to share the gospel with this Cuban doctor who had been raised in a socialist country where children generally grow up not hearing the gospel or, if they hear the gospel, they are taught there is no God. I thought, "Why bother? He has grown up being taught there is no God. How can I, in this brief encounter, overcome years of indoctrination of atheism?" Yet, the Holy Spirit prompted me to share with him and so I did.

I shared the gospel using the Evangecube. This is a small evangelism tool that looks somewhat like a rubric cube but unfolds in various ways to show pictures that go along with the gospel story. As you relay the message of man's sin, Jesus' substitutionary death to pay sin's penalty and His resurrection conquering sin and death, it will show pictures that go along with the story. Most cultures learn by storytelling, and this can be a very effective way to communicate across cultures and language barriers. I also felt led to focus on his medical knowledge of the intricacies of the human body and creation that points to the God of creation.

After presenting the gospel, I asked him if he believed this and wanted to surrender his life to Christ. He was silent for several moments, then turned to me and said, "I believe this and want to commit my life to Jesus Christ." It was my joy and honor to lead Julio in a prayer of confession and acceptance of Jesus Christ as his Savior.

When Julio "no showed" me, I almost missed the divine appointment God had set for him! How is it that we struggle to let go of the worldly ways of our Western culture where punctuality and productiveness have such a high value that we can let that place a priority in our day over God's work? His timing can often seem too slow or inefficient. Learning to let this go on the mission field can be an important yet difficult lesson for all of us. And hopefully, it is one we bring back home with us.

Fortunately, our national host was able to follow up with Julio and reported that he joined a local congregation and was continuing to grow in his faith. My hope upon hearing this was that when Julio returned to Cuba he would be going back as a missionary to his medical colleagues who were not yet Christ-followers.

I still don't like missed appointments in my practice. However, this experience taught me to look beyond a missed appointment and be more sensitive to GOD's divine appointments in my dental practice, both in the U.S. and when I am serving on a mission team.

## A True Dad
### Frank Imbarrato, MD

Years ago, GHO descended upon the southern Honduran town of El Paraiso for a healthcare mission trip. The local community was thrilled to have such an event in their small town. They closed the schools in the town, and we used one of them for our clinic. We had a large team of about 50 people, not counting interpreters.

The first day, as usual, brought huge crowds. There were throngs of children as they were off from school and wanted to come to see the "Americans." They hung out around the clinic each day and enjoyed spending time with team members who reciprocated with playing ball, Frisbee, blowing bubbles, kicking soccer balls or helping them practice their English. During lunch breaks during the week, some of us were introduced to their family members by being invited into their homes.

The team talked about Jesus to the children, and they loved the Evangecube. The children would sing songs for the team and would constantly want to spend time with team members whenever an opportunity presented itself. A core group of about 20 to 30 children never left the clinic all week. They lived in the local neighborhood and were a constant presence in and among the team. At the end of the week, several children asked if they could write letters to us once we left town. They had photos taken with us and a few of us gave our home addresses to them, never expecting or anticipating ongoing correspondence with children who ranged from eight to 12 years old. The children became so bonded to the team that it was traumatic for them when the bus pulled away.

As the buses departed town and pulled away from the school on Friday afternoon, the children ran alongside of the bus yelling and shouting and even weeping as they could not keep up with the bus after it sped away. It was a glorious trip, and there was much fruit in serving in the town and sharing the love of Jesus throughout the week. We fondly spoke of the children who were so touched by the team and the team came to love the children. These are moments when you consider that if such deep attachments develop in such a short period of time, if "when helping hurts," whether these children will be positively or negatively impacted by such an event in their lives.

About a month later, a letter arrived at our home from a 10-year-old named Cris. It was mailed about three and a half weeks earlier, but it took a long time to arrive in New York. I remembered him well, as he was one of the quieter children among the multitude we met. I had an opportunity to meet his mom and his two brothers. His mom volunteered at the clinic during the week and served the team with dedication and great fondness. She had invited us to her home one day, which was down the block from the clinic. She treated us to coffee, tea and cookies. She was solid in her faith and was active in the local church. The boys loved Jesus, which was a great reflection of their mother's devotion to the Lord and to the boys. Cris' dad abandoned the family a few years earlier for drugs and other women.

Cris' letter was simple and relatively short, but he talked about how much Jesus blessed him and how thankful and blessed he and the town were to have us come and serve them. He talked about going back to school after we left town and how all the children would smile, laugh and tell stories of the Americans. Knowing some Spanish, I was able to return a note to Cris and spoke of the gift it was to the team to be able to serve and share the love of Jesus with them.

Without fail, at least once a month, a letter would arrive from Cris letting me know he was praying for me and my family. He would share very little about what was going on in his life or family, only wanting me to know that he loved Jesus, that Jesus was caring for him and his family and that he was praying for us. I remember once writing him back and asking him if there was anything he needed or could use. Over a period of many weeks, he responded that his sneakers were badly worn and had holes in them. In the next letter I sent, I needed to know the size of his foot to get him some sneakers. A few weeks later, I received a letter and a drawing of his foot where he traced his foot on a piece of paper to show me how big his foot was.

The relationship continued, mostly because of his faithfulness in writing and keeping in touch. He would eventually share life details about his family, mom, grandmother, brothers, school and church. By the time he was 13 or 14, he would occasionally go to the internet café and send me emails instead of paper letters. I was pleased to have more efficient communication. He never asked for anything!

Over the next few years, life became more difficult for Cris, his mom and his brothers. Cris needed to move in with his grandmother for a couple of years. Cris loved his mom and missed her terribly. She and his brothers moved in with his aunt. He continued to pray for her and his family. He continued to go to church and eventually started working in the local pharmacy while he was in secondary school. I would ask about his mom and dad regularly. Sadly, he would relate that his dad continued to be absent.

Cris graduated secondary school and wanted to go to university to study and get a degree. He enrolled in a local university and graduated in four years with a degree in Turismo. While he was in university, I was reunited with Cris in Nicaragua where he joined us on a GHO trip about five years ago. He helped in the clinic and often would have tears in his eyes remembering when he was the boy running around spending time with team members. He gave his testimony to the GHO team, and the team and Cris were touched to the core knowing God has had His hand on this boy from the time GHO showed up in his hometown.

Cris' mom developed a brain tumor but was able to have treatment and is currently in remission. Cris' dad died last year from HIV, and Cris wept bitterly at his funeral. He still grieves his dad's death and says that regardless of what the past held for him, he loved his dad and misses him.

Cris has joined us on two more GHO trips over the last few years; one in El Salvador and one more in Nicaragua. He loves to serve and has become friends with different team members and keeps in touch with them on social media. He has remained a faithful Christ follower and loves Jesus. Cris is now 25 years old and moved to Mexico about two years ago to get a job and work. Employment in Honduras is almost impossible. He has remained employed and works hard. He supports his mom the best he can and still rarely ever asks for much. God did supply him with some support for university and also for his mom's healthcare. But overall, Cris has blessed my life in his walk with the Lord and his testimony more than my wife and I could ever bless him. He calls me his true dad, and I am privileged to carry that banner.

## Free in Christ
### Dr. Rani, MD
### National Partner, Indonesia

I always love the opportunity to prepare and be involved in GHO mission trips. Once, we decided to go to this remote island where there are no believers. To go there, we have to drive inland then to the coast and spend the night there before we cross over the next morning. This is one of the most difficult and challenging trips, in my opinion. But somehow, the preparation went smoothly. Being on many mission trips before, that raised an alarm for me because when you do God's work, the enemy will surely try to stop you.

So, we set out and camped for the night in this small village. That night, I wasn't able to sleep, regardless of how tired I was. Every time I tried to close my eyes, I would have this vivid dream or vision that there is a gathering of the enemies, ready for battle. There were many of them and they were making loud noises and they were laughing, in a mean way. So, I would wake up and pray and try to sleep again and the same dream/sight would happen again or continue. Over and over again. Around 1 a.m., one of the other national partners woke me up. The local authority came to question us and forbid us from crossing over. And I thought, "This is it." I spent the morning trying to get permission by contacting many people while friends in the main city did everything they could to help. By midday, it was obvious we would not be able to cross over.

By God's grace, we were able to share the gospel to the boatmen and the family who helped us in that village. This included a small boy who was nine or 10 years old, small for his age. He spoke in his native language, which was translated to the Indonesian language and then to English. He received Jesus as his Savior that day. What makes him special is that he is a slave. And yes, human slavery still exists! On our island it is part of the culture. When asked what his wishes were, he replied, "To go to school." He wasn't allowed to study or go to school, perhaps because the master doesn't see the benefit of that. His parting words to us were, "Thank you so much for coming into this village. I am not able to see what the outer world is like, but you all come here and show me what the world is like."

Many would call that trip a fail. And while I had over 600 people from the remote island in my mind, perhaps God had that little boy from that village in His mind from the beginning. We didn't get to minister to 600 or so non-believers, but we got to minister to this little boy and his small family (all of them are slaves).

When I recalled the dream or vision I had the night before, I was reminded of Luke 4:18-19, "The Spirit of the Lord is upon Me, because He anointed me to bring good news to the poor. He has sent Me to proclaim release to captives, and recovery of sight to the blind, to set free those who are oppressed, to proclaim the favorable year of the Lord" (NASB). I am convinced, once again, that one soul, big or small, young or old, slave or free, is precious to Christ. That day, the slave boy was set free. Though he's still a slave to his earthly master, he is free in Christ. Free indeed!

## Nothing is Impossible with God
*Andy Sanders, MD*

It is nice in life to be "in control." As healthcare professionals, we are used to that feeling, the feeling of being in charge, being confidant, knowing how to handle challenging situations. In Scripture, though, we find numerous admonitions to "trust in the Lord." It is not easy to turn from trusting self and our visible resources to trusting God and His unseen tools and promises. One of the blessings I have found being part of a healthcare mission team is being faced with many situations where my efforts and abilities are not enough, situations that turn into glorious opportunities to "trust in the Lord."

One of the challenges that face healthcare teams is with the supplies they need to carry overseas at times. Sometimes these extra supplies can fit in the team luggage. Sometimes extra bags can be brought on board with a little extra payment. The luggage is something we can plan out and, with a little creativity, organization and extra money, this logistic problem is usually solved.

But there are times when the luggage issue is an overwhelming issue that provides an insurmountable obstacle to the mission of the team. At times, we have been placed in situations with luggage where we are completely unable to solve the problems our supplies have caused. In these times, as much as we tried to trust in our abilities, we were left looking and trusting in Him. Two supply memories come quickly to mind.

One such luggage impossibility arose with a team I was taking to Indonesia. We had, as all teams do, been working diligently for a few months getting prepared individually and as a team for the mission that would soon be starting. The team was ready to go. Logistics has been prepared down to the appropriate weight of all our cases. However, unknown to us, but known to Another, an earthquake was about to come. That is, a real earthquake. A week before our departure, a large and devastating earthquake struck Indonesia, right where we were to serve. Suddenly there was a great need for trauma supplies. The team put the word out to hospitals, and we were blessed with an incredible outpouring of support. Supplies flooded into our team to take to Indonesia with us. A great blessing—and an insurmountable problem. We now had a mountain of boxes and heavy crates to bring with us! All of our logistical planning and all of our "extra money" were useless to solve this "dilemma." However, four years before, the Lord had begun solving this problem for our team, long before we even knew we were a team. The earthquake that was new at this time had been known in detail by our Sovereign team leader long before. On an earlier team I was leading to Eastern Europe four years earlier, we had a few extra bags of supplies. I asked the agent at the counter if they could allow these bags to be checked without the extra fees. The agent said she would need to call a supervisor over. The airline supervisor was very friendly, and very interested in what we were doing, but apologetically said she was unable to go against the airline's guidelines and we needed to pay for the additional few bags. However, she gave me her card and said if there is a need we know of ahead of time in the future to please call her and she would do what she could do to help us.

So, four years later and faced with this great mass of supplies, I found that card and called this friendly supervisor. She was still with the airline, was still very eager to help us and she went to work on our problem. On the day of our travel, I received word from her that all had been arranged. When we arrived at the airport with our luggage and our mountain of supplies, the airline was waiting for us. We were greeted, thanked for what we were doing, and without anything being weighed, our mountain of cargo was taken from us and was later waiting for us in Indonesia. In all my countless airlines trips, only one airline official has ever given me a business card. What had been merely a "chance" encounter, nothing that appeared out of the ordinary, had actually been the Lord at work. The Lord knew that four years later there would be a team looking to Him, trusting in Him. And He had everything under control!

The other memory takes me back to Europe. We had prepared to bring a healthcare team to Siberia. A few trips had been made already in preparation, and finally the time had come to bring an entire team to the middle of Siberia. Once again, we had everything planned out just right. We maximized our weight allowances and with two heavy suitcases each and a heavy carry-on, our team left the U.S. I had been told our bags would go directly to Siberia. All was under control.

However, to our shock, the bags all came off the plane in Moscow. We had to retrieve them and check them through on the next flight to Siberia. This was a small airline that allowed only one 20-pound bag per person. As a team, we had well over 1,000 pounds beyond what they allowed. The airline workers at the gate were firm (and non-smiling) and would not consider any help with our dilemma. The expense for all the extra weight was far beyond what our team had. Returning to the U.S. appeared to be a very real likelihood. My co-leader, though, excused himself, saying he was going to see what could be done and for us to be praying. He was gone for more than 30 minutes. When he returned, he had with him a smiling Russian airline official. They had become friends, and this new friend was eager to help our team. Much to the frustration of the airline workers at the gate, he stood there and made sure all our extra luggage was carried onto the plane without difficulty and without any expense. Our impossible logistical dilemma had been solved in a way we would have considered impossible. I would strongly suspect that in that entire airport, there would at the most be only one person with a heart to stop what he was doing, go out of his way, exert his authority and solve this dilemma. And the One who said to our team, "Trust in me," led my co-leader right to that unknown man whom He had prepared for us.

Impossibilities, absolute impossibilities, will face us at times on these teams. It is always a bit of a challenge to our flesh to turn from trusting self to trusting God. But, oh, what a joy to see Him work and to witness His sovereignty over man and circumstances. And, personally, what a blessing to see that we have returned to our lives back home with a little less hold on our own control and a tighter embrace on His, with a little less trust in "me" and a growing trust in "Him."

"Trust in the Lord with all your heart, and do not lean on your own understanding. In all your ways acknowledge him, and he will make straight your paths" (Proverbs 3:5-6, ESV).

## Preach to the Choir
*Dr. Rani, MD*
*National Partner, Indonesia*

GHO came to serve on an island in Indonesia. As their national partner, we were hosting them and serving in a medical clinic in one of the remote villages. We had a lot of patients who wanted to be seen. As usual, I work as a physician with the team and see patients by myself since I don't require an interpreter. The pastor of that village, a lady, came to me. I listened to her complaints, asked questions, examined her, diagnosed her ailments and prescribed the medications to help her physical complaints. Then came the most important part (for me), which is when I get to ask every patient how they would like me to pray for them.

Now, most people assume that pastors and preachers are surely Christians, but I have learned never to assume someone's salvation. So, instead of asking her first what she would like me to pray for her, I said to her, "I know the Bible is what you probably preach every Sunday and what you talk about to people when you see them or do any kind of service for them, but still, would you mind if I do it for you now? Tell you again about our Savior and what He does for us and how we can be reconciled to Him?" She said, "Yes."

So, the gospel sharing began, followed by prayers. She cried the whole time, sobbing, not caring that the members of her congregation were there too. And she said to me, "Thank you so much. This is the first time ever in my life someone told me the gospel for me and ask to pray for me." For almost 20 years in her service, she was always the one doing those things. It became a habit, and she didn't realize how badly she needed that. As national partners, when we prayerfully decide which village to go to, we consider a lot of information, mostly the numbers of non-believers. And yet, when God decided we should go to areas like this, for me, as always, it is a divine appointment. There are people He wants.

# JORDAN
## 30.5852° N, 36.2384° E

## Transforming Hearts on Mission
*Frank Imbarrato, MD*

GHO had entered into the refugee crisis early on and was sending teams to serve in the Middle East even before the mass exodus of refugees from Syria and Iraq in 2015. Once the flood of refugees hit in 2015, the governments and churches in the Middle East were overwhelmed. GHO had a relationship with a church in Amman, Jordan. This church was well established and had been serving refugees for several years prior to 2015. We had a relatively small team heading to Jordan that year, but it was the perfect size ordained by God because of different logistics.

Becky, a physician assistant, had called me and was interested in joining the team several months prior. She had served on the mission field in previous years, but she wanted to step out of her comfort zone and serve in a more difficult area. After a time of prayer, Becky was registered to serve with GHO for the first time in Ammon, Jordan.

Becky is a young single woman who is strong in faith, humble in spirit and knowledgeable of the Word. She was working for a urologist at the time and was unsure of her clinical skills for a mission clinic setting. She was encouraged she would do wonderfully well and God would provide for any and all deficiencies in each of us. We both live in the same area of the country, so we left from the same airport. Traveling together allowed us a time to get to know one another and to pray with each other.

The clinic was busy, and we were only limited in patient care by adequate interpreters who spoke the different dialects of Arabic. Out of respect for their different cultures, the church arranged for the Iraqi and Syrian patients to be seen on different alternating days. It made it a bit easier for the interpreters as well.

The team had wonderful opportunities to do home visits and serve a diverse population of demographics throughout the two weeks of clinic. There was a good blend of acute and subacute medical problems that made the week interesting and challenging. Becky did exceptionally well and especially fell in love with the Syrian women. The Holy Spirit provided frequent open doors to proclaim Jesus to these dear souls who were in bondage to Allah and the Islamic religion. It was encouraging to know the local church stood strong among the people to follow up on those touched by the gospel message and the love of Jesus.

When the time came to leave, Becky's heart was being ripped by love of the people and the passion to share the Good News of Jesus. It was bittersweet, as it usually is, leaving after a time of service with GHO and our national partners.

Life continued back in the U.S. once we arrived home. I kept in touch with several team members. Becky was struggling and had a restless spirit. As we continued to talk and pray over the next few months, Becky's heart continued to be drawn back to Jordan. She soon called me to celebrate and share the news that she was in contact with a mission organization and she would be heading to the mission field in God's proper timing.

After the customary time preparing for the mission field and all that is involved between training, fundraising, language school, etc., Becky was ready to launch back to Jordan as a full-time missionary. She was able to do her language training in-country in Ammon. The organization had recently had a church plant there in Jordan among the refugees, and Becky was to join the grassroots labors. Through her medical skills, she had doors open to her caring for woman and children in their homes and sharing the gospel. She dwells in the refugee community and is developing a reputation for one who loves and serves among the Syrians. Her Arabic is adequate, as she says she has a long way to go, but God is providing for any and all deficiencies.

She has now been serving the refugee population in Jordan for three years. God is using her in the church and among the young people. She is home on her first sabbatical. I recently had breakfast with her, and she relates her thanks to GHO and the open door the mission trip allowed for her. The holy Spirit used GHO and the mission trip to Jordan to transform a heart for His greater kingdom purposes. She praises God and gives Him all the glory for the work He is doing in Jordan. She celebrates Jesus for the kingdom work being done around the world and through GHO. May God continue to transform hearts though the ministry of GHO.

# KENYA
## 0.0236° S, 37.9062° E

## Anything, Anywhere, Anytime, Any Cost
### Herb Bromenshenkel, RPh

I was introduced to GHO by a friend who received an email of a trip to Kenya needing a pharmacist. I was interested since they needed a pharmacist and, though I had been on many missions, I had never served on a healthcare mission team before. Still, I had just gotten back from a relatively hard trip in Malawi, but I remembered the piece of paper in my billfold: "Anything, anywhere, anytime, any cost."

The thing about God is that He has a plan for each of our lives. We just have to be willing to walk with Him and trust Him. Each one is called differently, but if we walk with Him and trust Him, He will guide us down our path. I received Jesus Christ as my Savior when I was 22 years old. Unfortunately, it took me longer to make Him my Lord. I was in a church in Belize years later when I gave my first testimony. My testimony was horrible. I say that not from a false humility, as it truly was horrible. I remember the team leader saying, "That was different." I wasn't raised in a church that gave personal testimonies, so all of this was new for me, but I put my heart into the trip, to serve and seek Him in all ways.

Later that week, we had the opportunity to go to a prison. I was one of the few to be selected to go to the maximum-security section. I remember walking by the outside of each cell asking, "Do you know Jesus?" All of them would say yes, but I would go through the cube anyway. Then I came to a cell, and asked, "Do you know Jesus?" and the person said, "No, tell me about Him." I was crushed as I realized I could not tell him from my heart who Jesus was to me. All I could do was go through the script. I did not have the words to describe Jesus as my best friend. I did the best I could, got to the end of the row and walked down the stairs. Halfway between the levels, I stopped and prayed. I was desperate. I was asking God, "What am I doing here, why am I here?" I just failed telling someone who Jesus was from my heart. I then proceeded down to the bottom, and immediately a prisoner came up to me and I said, "Do you know Jesus?" He took my hand to shake it and with a smile, he proceeded to tell me for minutes who Jesus was. "He is the Lord, He is the Redeemer, He is the everlasting one, He is forever," and on and on. The whole time he talked he kept shaking my hand. My arms, back and legs were tingling with a pulsating power from this man. It was my first real, tangible, without a doubt experience from God. All I could say was "Yes, Yes, Yes!" I did not want to let go. I was changed that day.

Years later, I was asked to go Kenya with a group of six people who loved Jesus, not with a formal organization. Unfortunately, the pastor hosting us was deceitful in many ways and the area had much witchcraft. About a week into the trip, we ended the day with a spiritual battle that manifested as a team conflict in the middle of the night. We resorted to prayer. We prayed on our hands and knees as a team in a hallway. One member had a rosary, and although not a fan of the rosary, I grabbed the cross and held on. Someone received a word from God that there were evil spirits in the room where conflict had risen, and I was to go in first. I remember walking in the room. As I crossed the threshold my hands started to feel like they were burning. I raised my left hand and just started walking toward the closet. About halfway there, two people at once said, "There they go." I did not see anything, but two people had their spiritual eyes opened in that moment. Immediately following, one person had a vision of a verse. Literally, saw the verse notation Luke 6:10 and said, "We have to read it, right now!" "And after looking around at them all he said to him, 'Stretch out your hand.' And he did so, and his hand was restored" (Luke 6:10, ESV). I had not uttered a word to anyone that my hand had been burning. At that moment, when I read the verse, I could feel God throughout my entire body. Throughout these mission trips, God was teaching me, growing me. That trip provided me the most important lesson of my life: The words of John 15:4-5: "Abide in me, and I in you. As the branch cannot bear fruit by itself, unless it abides in the vine, neither can you, unless you abide in me. I am the vine; you are the branches. Whoever abides in me and I in him, he it is that bears much fruit, for apart from me you can do nothing" (ESV). I made a commitment that trip. I signed it, and to this day, many years later, I keep the piece of paper in my billfold. My commitment was: "Anything, anywhere, anytime, any cost."

The first mission trip I served on with GHO was that trip to Kenya. I worked as a pharmacist and really enjoyed the chance to use my training and skills on the mission field. The team leader knew of my background in evangelical missions and arranged for me to help conduct a pastor's training conference the following year. On my third GHO trip, we held a pastor's conference for 65 pastors in one town, 30 in another, some having traveled from other countries in Africa to join us. It was so clear as I was preparing. It was like God was saying, "All those other trips, the hard ones, easy ones, honest pastors, dishonest pastors, they were all to prepare you for these meetings." I remember one moment so clear. I was writing one of the talks, and I went out and cut off a stem from a tomato plant located on my deck and brought it into the room where I was preparing. The entire room was filled with the fragrance of a fresh tomato. I walked into the room the next morning, and there was nothing. The tomato stem had completely dried up and was crumbly, and the fragrance was completely gone. I knew God was reminding me that the only way to produce fruit was to be connected to the vine of Christ and the Holy Spirit's life within me.

I know the power of God on mission trips. Sometimes it seems He doesn't show up until the need is desperate, but He is always there. It may seem odd, but now, when preparing for a mission trip, my number one prayer isn't all the issues with logistics. It's praying for intimacy with His presence and His Holy Spirit to flow through me. For

I know, if I am in Christ, and He in me, His Spirit will provide all my needs.

## Choosing the Eternal Over the Temporary
*Phillip L. Aday, DDS*

Being a GHO team leader involves months of preparation and focus on budget, supplies, travel, local hosts and recruiting. The team leader gauges the personalities of the members, praying they comfortably connect with each other and can handle the challenges of healthcare missions. Then the fun part begins as team members travel from all over North America and meet either at the airport or at the mission destination.

Such was the case with a large team I was leading to Kenya. We were serving in the outskirts of Nairobi in Dandora, a slum to which I had led multiple teams. After two days of airline flights, we spent one day for recovery/team building before we began the healthcare outreach.

We were serving in a school in the middle of the slum and were given the entire facility for our ministry. The GHO team was very robust with three physicians, five dentists, two pharmacists, several nurses and several non-medical servants. I was confident our team could see hundreds of patients in this Kenyan slum where nearly everyone has limited access to medical, dental and pharmacy services. The team had come together cohesively. I was unaware of any personality issues among the team that could cause friction. Our medical director was a veteran and had made the necessary assignments in the medical area to ensure our patients were directed to the appropriate clinician. I was managing the dental area with veteran dentists on the team. Everyone knew what services we were offering and required very little supervision.

Dandora school is in a fenced compound and consists of multiple buildings arranged in a square with a large inner courtyard. The working plan was to limit access to the compound and use the classrooms around the courtyard as treatment areas for medical, dental and pharmacy. The courtyard and covered sidewalk would serve nicely as waiting areas as our patients queued up for treatment.

On Wednesday the team was about halfway through our final week. I had finished treating my last morning patient and decided I would make rounds to each of the treatment areas to see how the day was progressing. I saw patients sitting in chairs outside each treatment room waiting for their turn to see the doctor. Suddenly I saw an elderly man collapse just outside a treatment room. I called for help and immediately our doctors responded. They began to assess his condition. It was determined Jonah had made it past our compound "gatekeeper" not registered as a patient and was walking around the compound visiting.

Our medical staff determined Jonah had low blood pressure and discovered his mouth was full of blood. Upon questioning, he admitted to a lifetime of heavy alcohol use. The blood in his mouth was from ruptured esophageal varices. This condition often occurs in patients with advanced liver disease. Without lab studies it was impossible to fully diagnose Jonah's condition, but his past history indicated he was most likely in end stage liver disease with a very poor prognosis. Our medical director had been one of the team members who had responded when Jonah had collapsed and was still at his side as he lay on a pallet in one of the treatment rooms. She was the only OB/Gyn physician on the team and her services were in high demand. Jonah's condition was not imminently life threatening, his bleeding had stopped and his vitals were stable. With our limited medical resources, there was nothing else medically we could do for him.

After lunch I returned to the dental area to begin treating the afternoon patients. In the mid-afternoon between patients, I again walked around the compound to check how the day was progressing. I noted a long line of female patients waiting outside the treatment room designated for OB/Gyn care. I was surprised to find our medical director still sitting beside Jonah. My thought was, "Why are you still sitting with this man? He is stable, there is nothing we can do for him and you have patients waiting to be seen." I suggested she could assign one of our nurses to sit with Jonah, but truly felt he should be encouraged to go home. She said she wanted to stay with Jonah.

That afternoon while making rounds I admit I was disappointed that Jonah was still in the compound and our OB/Gyn doctor was still at his side instead of seeing her patients. The team finished and headed back to our hotel for dinner and our evening team meeting. This gives us a chance to address any problems encountered during the day and decide on any changes that need to be made. This is also a time for team members to share any special experiences we call "God sightings." After addressing some minor problems encountered during the day, this same doctor asked to share.

She explained how she stayed by Jonah's side most of the afternoon visiting with him about his medical condition and the likelihood he did not have many more days here on earth. As she established a rapport with Jonah, she shared the gospel with him, and he came to faith in Christ. At that moment I was convicted in my heart. I had focused on staying on track by meeting the physical needs of our patients and not having them wait too long to see our healthcare professionals. She had been sensitive to Jonah's spiritual condition and his eternal destiny.

This was a reminder to me that the primary mission of GHO teams is to share the gospel. Physical maladies will recur. Prescriptions will run out. Dental disease can be addressed temporarily, but fillings will fail. Everything a GHO team does medically and dentally is temporary, but if we share the gospel and a patient becomes a Christ-follower, their life is changed for eternity. May I never forget the example of this caring doctor who chose the eternal over the temporary.

## God Saved a Life That Day
*Tamara Norton, RN*

In 1977, World Bank and several other organizations took part in funding a project on the outskirts of Nairobi, Kenya, believing it would help improve the standard of living for its low-income citizens. The hoped-for building sites and potential work availability dissolved into what is now known as Dandora. Dandora can be seen from outer space and is one of two major solid waste and toxic dump sites in Nairobi today. It is among the world's largest populated dump sites surrounded by slums.

Approximately 40 years later, a small city surrounds the Dandora dump sites with immigrants, refugees and Kenyans living there. It continues to receive more than 2,000 tons of waste per day. The residents here are limited to low or no income. Many are only making enough money to exist for another day by being a "picker." They pay to pick through the garbage dumped every day to scavenge for something to sell, use or even eat.

The toxic smoke from nightly burning of trash is a primary cause of rampant respiratory and optical issues suffered by those residing in Dandora. The metal, cinder block, mortar or tar paper dwellings have poor to non-existent ventilation. Kinyago School in Dandora is a primary school home to hundreds of students. School is not free here. Sponsorship and support by the Kenya Children's Fund are imperative to this small school's survival. The students receive breakfast and lunch, as well as uniforms, and they are given groceries to take home on Fridays. This helps supplement their family's food supplies.

Kinyago Dandora is an unforgettable place. It's filled with smiling, grateful people who live very much on the fringe of life. However, all are surrounded by brick walls, razor wire, high crime, poverty and the smell of burning garbage. Being here will change your life forever. It will change it in a good way—a way that tells you that you have brought skills to the right place. These are not necessarily healthcare skills, but to be of help and be of service skills. You never know what you possess until the moment presents itself. The "MacGyver" skills, we call them. The way a team can help you cobble together what is needed to fix a bad situation. You do what is required.

I believe I am a good hard working and knowledgeable nurse, but I have always been a little afraid of working with children! They become sick quickly and go downhill quickly, before you can even tell what is wrong. I stay clear and point to the pediatric experts. Only God would put me in the path of a pediatric emergency! So, on a busy day at Dandora, it was not unusual for our small group to see hundreds of patients. It is always a little chaotic, but in an organized way, a thousand parts all moving together.

On this day, I saw a woman bringing a small wrapped bundle toward me, and I began to motion to the pediatric nurse. One of the teachers at the school, David, said simply, "No, look." When mom dropped the blanket back, I saw a small, limp, dusky infant. I have seen death previously, but I always knew it was coming. Time stood still, it seemed forever though perhaps only seconds passed. I am pretty sure I ran for my team leader who is also my favorite doctor. She was only a few steps away. We moved the mom, with baby in her arms, quickly to a private area. Along the way I saw and grabbed two startled students. I felt like I was yelling and running, though someone asked later, "How where you so calm?" God gave me calm in that moment.

As we unwrapped and began to assess the limp child, we recognized his shallow breathing and flaccid muscles as a critical situation. He had a slight fever, had been vomiting and had diarrhea for a week, and his mother stated he had not been able to nurse in the past 24 hours because he was too weak.

We all carry a "bag of tricks" with us when we travel. It may contain dressing supplies for wounds, tubing for an IV and even duct tape! You never know what you will need in a foreign country. My "bag" will always have a small bag of IV fluids, as I had learned the necessity of that long ago.

"Please, Jesus, please," were the words on all of our lips as I found a small catheter and the small bag of fluids. Dr. Trish knew just the spot to put some IV fluids just under the skin between his shoulder blades instead of doing a regular IV, which can be tricky in infants, even when they're not severely dehydrated. Within seconds the child began to improve quickly. Something interesting happens in these critical moments; colors become brighter, sounds change and events become like a tattoo on your brain. He took a sudden deep breath and screamed! It was the best thing we have ever heard. As we dropped the fluids into the tiny guy, the students holding on to the bag for dear life and applying pressure to the bag to "push" the fluids, we began to cry. God had brought light to the room! We were no longer afraid.

We "MacGyvered" some Pedialyte solution into a sterile glove after poking a hole in a finger with a needle and began to drip the solution into his mouth. If you have ever lived on a farm, you recognize this trick. Within a few minutes he was taking small sips, he would rest and look around, and then sip more as he laid in his mother's arms. He was kept in the clinic for about four hours since we wanted to make sure he had gotten plenty of fluids in orally as well as watch the subcutaneous fluids to assess they had been absorbed by his tiny body.

Things calmed down and we returned to all the other clinic happenings as the mom and baby slowly recovered. We prayed with her and asked that she watch him carefully, but we also asked her to please return to clinic the next day so we could check on him. The next day, she dutifully appeared showing off the smiling baby boy she carried on her back, his name "Brian."

In some languages, the name Brian translates as noble or strong, I go with strong because he and his mother certainly are. I pray for them even now that they have stayed safe and strong and continue to survive living in Dandora. God used our team to save that little boy's life. I believe God has plans for him, and I pray he is used mightily by the Lord one day. For his good and God's glory.

## God's Calling
*Tamara Norton, RN*

How many times a day do I thank Him? Not nearly enough—we take so much of what we have for granted. Life would often be less stressful, and we could be satisfied, if we lived a life of gratitude and thankfulness. "In everything give thanks; for this is the will of God for you in Christ Jesus" (1 Thessalonians 5:18, NASB).

# GOD SIGHTINGS

The lack of gratitude and thankfulness is easily "fixed," though. Go on a GHO journey. It's not a "trip," but it is a journey. And I promise you will come home praising His name as you are filled with gratitude. It will also be filled with self-discovery, as what is truly important will soon come to light in your life.

The phrase, "I get much more from the mission trip than I give," is not uncommon and very real. You will come home changed, often with a greater understanding of the world and how others struggle to survive in it, along with the realization that we are not so very different. Everyone wants the same things we do: a safe place to live, enough food to feed a family and a better life for their children.

You don't have to be in the presence of those you are there to serve very long to see the hand of God and His blessings. Yes, you see great poverty and sadness. You also see hard work, kindness and love for the Lord. I am amazed how little I think they have, yet they are grateful. They have a much bigger heart for Jesus than I feel I will ever be capable of. In many ways they are richer than I am, especially in thanksgiving and prayer. I listen to the stories of war, injury, poverty and atrocities they have witnessed, yet they express gratitude for their very lives.

On my second mission trip in Kenya, we traveled to a beautiful coffee plantation area in the southwestern mountains of Kisumu. When I saw the relatively small town and even smaller clinic, I wondered if our team of more than 20 would overwhelm them. My answer came on the first day as we drove down the rutted red road—I saw people, then more people, then a sea of people. As we drove into the clinic site, we were blessed with smiles, waves and applause. Not the greeting I normally get!

In short order, the local church leaders and guards with the help of our team organized the patients and clinic spaces the best we could. We began to see patients for general medical, dental and eye screenings. I had served previously with the team leader and several other team members. Respect and flexibility are keys to a great mission team relationship.

I was working in the triage area helping to direct patients. I don't think we had been working very long when I heard a scream come from just outside the compound in a large coffee field at the back of the building. I have worked as an ICU nurse for 20 years so somehow, one scream did not startle me. I thought, probably just a kid playing. Another scream and a young Kenyan woman came running for help for her friend.

A young college student on our team offered to run back to see if she could help. My mind moved instantly to my next task; the young girl next in line and the grandfather waiting with her. The young girl had a rash on her face that our dermatologist could easily care for. It was the grandfather who captured my heart immediately. He smiled a beautiful African "welcome" smile. He offered the frequently heard, "God bless you." And he stepped forward with pride.

He walked with two canes and had no legs below his knees. His best suit was spotless and worn with polished brown loafers. His loafers were worn proudly on the stumps of his legs but pointed backward. I am sure I was smiling but also staring when he asked me, "Do you like my shoes?" His name was Moses, and he lost both of his legs a few inches below the knees in a farm accident when he was much younger. He had no choice but to "figure it out" with the Lord's help. After his stumps healed, he wore tire tread on his knees to work. He put rocks in the toes of the shoes to help with his balance. He soon realized wearing his shoes backward helped his balance. Backward was better! His friend intricately carved him the most beautiful short hardwood canes and he was set to go. Moses told me God had blessed him with health and a beautiful Christian family. "And we know that God causes all things to work together for good to those who love God, to those who are called according to His purpose" (Romans 8:28, NASB). He inspires me to this day! I hope to meet him again, even if the next time I see Moses is in heaven. I'm sure he will be wearing his best shoes!

I had forgotten about the scream in the field until our young team member arrived back. She was sweating and glowing. The screams were the sudden delivery of a healthy baby girl, delivered in a coffee field in the Kenyan mountains on a sunny summer day. The team member had held the mother's hand and coached her all through the delivery. All was well! I have a picture of the proud mother and a beautiful baby wrapped in a blanket given to her by a team member who "happened" to have brought two baby blankets to give away. The mother asked to name the baby Marisa after the young team member who stayed with her, who held her hand.

Today, four years later, Marisa has become a nurse and is working in labor and delivery. God showed her a calling that day in Kenya. We often never know until much later what the Lord will reveal to us or what He will give us to be grateful for. Just another quiet GHO clinic day. Send me back, Jesus. I miss those days so.

## He Alone is Worthy
*Catherine N. Osiemo*
*National Partner, Kinyago Dandora Schools, Kenya*

Early in the years when GHO began coming to Kenya to serve with the Kinyago Dandora school, we ran our clinic in Namanga the first week. While they were there working, the team decided to show the Jesus film in the evening, lasting to around 8 p.m. What amazed me most about that was their dedication to doing this after working all day in their medical clinic and the endless, tedious work.

There was a Muslim woman who continued coming to the clinic site to watch this film every evening. Near the end of the clinic, she decided to be saved, accepting Jesus as her Lord and Savior. This is particularly dangerous for Muslim women, and we cautioned her to be secretive about this with her family, as we were afraid they would hurt or reject her. The local pastors in her area decided to follow up with her to be sure she was okay and to encourage her in her new faith. They reported that she continued to attend weekday meetings and fellowship. She was not able attend Sunday church, or she would have alerted her family. She continued to grow in her faith in Jesus.

When GHO came back to that same area of Kenya the following year, she came to the clinic. She testified to the team members on how she was faring. The team was very grateful to hear she was doing well, continuing in her faith, and they encouraged her. The team took up a small, unplanned collection of money for her and gave her $15 to use as she needed.

Later during the mission trip, when the days are long and the team started to fatigue, the team members made their way to the guest house after the Jesus films were over. The team finally had the chance to eat dinner and begin their short evening team meeting, including praise and worship, a devotion and sharing God sightings from the day. The owner of the Namanga hospital came driving fast to the guest house. He was requesting the GHO doctors come and assist him with an emergency. There was an accident nearby. They were rushed by ambulance to the Namanga hospital, as he wanted our team's assistance.

When he approached me, I was hesitant and told him the doctors were extremely tired but felt that I should allow him to speak to the team. When the team leader heard him speak, he asked the group if any of the doctors would be willing to go and see if they could help. Their ability to help would of course be dependent on the injuries sustained. To my surprise, they all jumped up and were willing to go!

It happened that one of the ladies I was sharing a room with was one of the people who went, along with her father. I had to wait until midnight for her to return and hear how the patients were. I have never forgotten the selflessness of the GHO team members and the way they use their life and skills to help God's people around the world. He alone is worthy of it all and may God receive all the glory! Amen.

# Jane
### *Ann M. Craig, MD*

I am a pediatrician who has served in Kenya numerous times with the Kinyago Dandora School, our GHO national partner for Kenya. Jane was the school's headmistress, and she made a tremendous impact on me. As I served with her on mission trips to Kenya over the years, Jane became more than a national partner to me. She became a friend. She was a God sighting to me and our GHO teams.

Jane loved bright colors, bouncy music, children and Jesus. I will never forget her hearty laugh and broad smile. She spoke English fluently but with just a little bit of a drawl on top of her Kenyan accent. Jane was as enthusiastic in her worship as she was with the children. She subtly complained that our American worship songs were dreary and slow. So, when we finally found an upbeat song that everyone on the team could sing and do hand motions for, I immediately had the team share it with Jane. She loved it and asked us to sing it every day.

What a passion she had for the children! Her passion was joined by her practical nature, so each school break, the kids were sent home to their families with a generous food supply. Even so, the children would come back from their month-long holidays thinner and sicker. The staff would go to work preparing breakfast and hot lunch for those students. Jane and her army were determined to care for those kids as well as possible. When we visited a hospital on our team travels and learned about a filtration system that could provide clean water, Jane got the details she could try to bring it back to her kids.

Jane knew every one of those kids. Her door was open to them, and I learned she visited the families in the slum where they lived. I remember her patience with one primary student named Lucy who hung out near Jane constantly. We knew Lucy was chronically ill with ascites and jaundice, but it was Jane who finally took her for an HIV test and Lucy's AIDS was diagnosed. Jane made sure Lucy got her anti-retroviral therapy. With sadness, Jane told me of Lucy's death a year or two later.

Jane was determined that her students would succeed. Initially, they had only a primary school, up through eighth grade, or Class 8 as they call it in Kenya. With Jane's vision, leadership and persuasion, an old factory was purchased and outfitted as a secondary school. She proudly took the GHO teams on a tour of the facility every year and inspired both Americans and Kenyans to donate to the project. Even now, students from that school go on to college or technical positions, well prepared. One has even been elected to parliament.

Jane was a hard person to say no to. I loved her, and when she admired my favorite t-shirt from home, I knew what to do. I wonder where in Kenya that shirt is now.

Over the years, I learned that Jane was a cancer survivor. I've always assumed it was breast cancer, but in Kenya, you don't chat about such things. I knew it came back and one year, it was evident that my dear Jane was failing. I made plans to arrive before the rest of the team so I would have a little time to visit with my friend. Tragically, we lost her three weeks before I arrived back. I spent those extra days in Nairobi mourning, sharing memories with others who had loved her. Dandora has never been the same since. No one can quite fill Jane's shoes. I can still hear her laugh, and I miss it. I miss you, my dear Jane.

## Medical Diagnosis and Spiritual Healing
*Catherine N. Osiemo*
*National Partner, Kinyago Dandora Schools, Kenya*

I work for Kinyago Dandora Schools in Kenya as the Sponsorship Director, and we are happy to be one of the national partners for GHO. We are very grateful for Ginger Palm, CEO and President of Kenya Children's Fund, which works to help support our schools and played a part in our partnership with GHO. We always look forward to when a mission team is coming! It requires much work and preparation, but it is always a tremendous blessing as well. We move the team around in our country the first week they are here to strategic areas where the gospel is not known or perhaps commonly misunderstood. Once we feel that area is reached, we then move on to other areas in my country. The second week the GHO team serves in Dandora, which is a world-famous slum area just outside of Nairobi on which a town has been built. This is one of the poorest of the poor areas. Our small Christian schools are located here and educate the children in this area using a sponsorship model to assist in funding. We schedule the GHO mission team during a school break, which allows the team to use the school here for their clinic site, and most of the interpreters are teachers in our school.

One year we had a woman who came to the Dandora clinic with a child who had a recently fractured arm. Before reaching the registration desk, she fell down off her chair while the child was sitting on her lap, and she landed on the child. The child cried so much it brought attention to them among the crowd of patients. They were taken to the school clinic area, and after some assessment it was determined this young mother had epilepsy. It was suspected she had a seizure, which had caused her to fall on the child at home injuring her arm. Interestingly, she developed this while in her rural home, and they believed someone had bewitched her.

Her parents had taken her to an herbalist and to local and traditional prophets with no success. Her family decided to send her to a family relative in Nairobi in hopes they could send her to other prophets to pray for her. The GHO team doctor who saw her referred her to a hospital in Nairobi. The team collected the $30 needed to pay the hospital fee. They wanted her to have an x-ray and bring the results back to the clinic. We suggested it would be better if we gave her half the money to start; that way, she would be sure to come by our clinic for the other half afterward and bring us the results.

She did return to pick up the rest of the money with a splint on her arm and the x-ray result. The team doctor was happy that she got the appropriate treatment. The mom was then referred for counseling with Pastor David, who works with the school and also with the GHO team every year.

In Nairobi, we realized she went to another prophet for prayers and it took some time, but Pastor David was able to convince her that she was not bewitched but had developed epilepsy. She was advised to live with another adult in the house instead of living alone with her two little children for security reasons in case she falls again with a seizure. We wanted her and her children to be safe. Through counseling, she was also advised that she should stop wasting her time on local prophets and instead look for medical assistance regarding her seizures and taught her about the gospel message and praying to Jesus.

There are still many people in my country who continue to believe in witchcraft. But thank God, through GHO she learned she was not bewitched but had developed a medical condition. She has been seen around the area and those who have seen her testify she is increasing her weight and is looking healthier. She has less stress now because she learned that there were not people who were looking at her with bad eyes and did not like her.

I know serving cross-culturally is a challenge! We are grateful that GHO comes alongside us and we can work together to reach our poor community with a healing touch and the gospel of Jesus Christ. It helps us reinforce good health to our community while explaining a medical condition and not fearing witchcraft or other black magic. We love GHO and continue to pray for them. Many of the team members over the years have become sponsors for children in our school, which continues the blessings for these poor children and their families. It is a blessing to be able to reach out to our community and know others around the world are reaching out as well.

## On My Own
### Kenya 2018 Team Member

I enjoy writing and sharing about the wonderful things I have seen the Lord do, about the wonderful people I meet and about the incredible life experiences we share on the mission field. What is harder to talk about is the times I know I failed. "My flesh and my heart may fail, but

God is the strength of my heart and my portion forever" (Psalm 73:26, NASB). Times when I know I allowed myself to come to someone without God by my side. Knowing I needed to ask Him for help, but somehow unable to do so. Vanity comes to mind; I can do this!

Is it possible to feel repulsion toward someone and still love the Lord? Is it possible to see reflected in someone's eyes the truth that you have not given your best? And feel guilt for that, even after you have turned it over to God and asked forgiveness? Yes, I have to believe so. I have been told, "It happens," but I try for it not to be me. I worry I have failed that person and so they have not seen the Lord in me or what He can do for them. I was a bad example of Christ to someone, I failed. I know this never happens to others of faith, right?

My failure came in a subtle way, in a quiet way and a surprising way. It was my own fault. I thought I could handle it alone. I found out later her name was Miriam, which honestly made it all the worse. God's Miriam sang and danced; this woman could not even walk. She hobbled. She hobbled in the most crooked of ways, wrapped under a smelly blanket that covered her head to toe. She appeared short but that was because her previously broken bones had never been set or treated. They had healed in disastrous curves and edges, making her unable to stand properly or move her arms freely. A motorcycle accident and no money for the hospital or doctor left her crippled in a cruel and painful position.

Miriam came to me with bruises on her face and arms, scrapes on elbows and knees. She had rocks hailed on her by the wife of a man she had slept with so she could have money to feed herself. I noticed even the workers helping us shied away from her. She was crumpled and lost. She had so many needs. I wanted to give her healthcare, but also food, shelter, warmth and safety. She needed Jesus. Looking back, I don't think I gave her Him either.

I felt a darkness I have never felt before as we prayed with her. I felt the words were empty. We had some medicine to offer her for her wounds, but nothing else we had could really reach the depth of what she needed. She scampered away as all eyes followed her. I felt guilt.

I also felt shame. Why had I not offered her food, a fresh blanket, a warm cloth? Offered some kindness? Something about her made me feel empty and worthless.

I went to the gate to stop her, bring her back, spend time with her. She was gone, and I realized I had not touched her. My hands so ready to touch and comfort had not reached out for her. To this day I wonder why, and I see her in my mind's eye often.

I do know this, that encounter and my failure that day changed me. It has pushed me to go again and again to the medical mission field. Made me more aware of my own weakness in helping in my own strength. It is a constant reminder of how easily darkness can enter your spirit and we must fight to keep it at bay. I have prayed that one day, somehow, I can make up for that moment. Perhaps that is its value. Lessons learned can be hard. I remind myself constantly that I need the help of Jesus every day, and to remember how easy it is to ask, and His presence will be with me.

## The Wrong Line
### Rodney Bahnson, Non-medical Servant

I am a retired businessman and have never done any medical work or volunteer service. And honestly, I never really thought about it. A friend of mine suggested I volunteer to serve on a GHO mission trip, explaining they often need more non-medical or logistic servants to help their teams. So, after praying about it, I emailed a team leader and said, "I am an old, retired businessman with no medical experience. Can you use an old guy like me on your team?" She responded that yes, she could use my help. So, I signed up to go with GHO to Kenya.

Serving on the GHO team in Kenya was a blessing to me. We served in a more rural area the first week, then got to enjoy a safari over the weekend before returning to Nairobi for our second week. It was definitely stepping outside my comfort zone as I served in different areas of the clinic. One day I was assigned to evangelism, which I had never done before. I was nervous about doing this since I had never shared the gospel before. I know I wasn't eloquent or able to share the gospel perfectly, but I sure did learn to love the opportunity to tell them about Jesus. And I really learned to love that Evangecube!

During our second week of clinic, we were already running out of reading glasses. The team leader decided to limit the age of patients who could go to the eye clinic to those older than 35 years of age, since younger people don't tend to need glasses to see close up and that is all we had. I was working in the eye clinic that day and a 15-year-old girl somehow got in the reading eyeglass line. Not only that, but she had also waited in this line for three hours before I saw her. I thought to myself, "I wonder how she got in this line? They aren't allowing younger patients." But since she had already waited, I went ahead and saw her. As expected, it turned out she needed distance glasses, which we did not have. I told her this and she was very nice about it. I also asked her about her faith. She was not a Christian and wanted to hear more about Jesus. I was able to take my time and share the gospel with her. She accepted Jesus as her Savior that day. We rejoiced together. I guess I know who helped her slip in the reading eyeglass waiting line!

It is always amazing to see how God works in and through our clinics. I have been back to Africa with GHO several times now, and I have grown from one anxious about doing evangelism to asking if I can do evangelism some days. God takes what we have to offer, even a wisdom-aged man sharing the gospel in a small school in Africa, and increases His kingdom for eternity. Praise God for His indescribable gifts!

# LEBANON

## Plant, Water, Harvest
*Janelle Carbary, PA*

"Jesus did many other things as well. If every one of them were written down, I suppose that even the whole world would not have room for the books that would be written" (John 21:25, NIV). When I started to write some of what God did in Lebanon, this was the verse that came to mind. He has done so much in many people's lives all around the world, and I feel humbled to even write a small part.

Lebanon was the first time I served people in the form of a health-care mission trip. I was so awed by how we can provide a degree of physical healing to people, but more importantly I learned that healthcare can be used as a conduit to bring the "living water" of the gospel to people. As we had the opportunity to share the gospel, I saw John 4:37, "For in this case the saying is true, 'One sows and another reaps'" (NASB), come to life in two situations on the last day of clinic. This was never truer than on that day.

One of my first patients was a lady who had been attending women's meetings hosted by the missionaries we were working with. She had been attending these meetings and hearing the gospel for many months, but she continued to feel guilty about her past and ashamed to discuss these things. In a larger group setting, she was able to slip away, but internally she was in the midst of a personal wrestling match. The Holy Spirit led me to talk about the women at the well as described in John 4. As Jesus extended grace to that women in the Bible, I saw the Holy Spirit whisper a "knowing of her past" to my patient and the revelation of grace reached the windows of her heart. She gave her life to Jesus with tear-filled eyes in that moment.

Toward the later part of the day, there was a young lady who I met who was of Muslim faith and had traveled as a refugee from Syria. She had the sweetest smile and countenance. After we discussed her medical concerns, I had asked if she was interested in hearing about Jesus. She looked back at me with a dumbfounded look and said she had never heard of Jesus. I can honestly say I have never started at square one with somebody. In many cultures, people have heard of the person Jesus in relation to a religion or church. With the help of my amazing translator who also loved Jesus, we started from the very beginning. As we navigated through Adam and Eve and sin all the way through the birth and death of Jesus Christ, this young girl had her mouth open almost the whole time and continued saying, "Wow." When she finally heard the entirety of the gospel, she asked in many different ways, "What does all of this cost?" She was so surprised and shocked to learn she didn't have to pay for Jesus to forgive her sins and love her. She struggled to understand that the gospel was a free gift. She did not accept Jesus into her heart that day, but I saw a child-like excitement as she walked away from the clinic because she had heard of the love of Jesus for the first time. She agreed to come to the women's meetings being held by the missionaries, but in that moment the Lord imparted to me a valuable lesson.

These two ladies are the essence of GHO mission trips in a way. The first lady I met was already so open to the gospel because of the time and effort others had spent investing in her. So, at the right timing, I asked if she wanted to accept Jesus into her heart and it was an easy yes. The second lady had never heard the gospel, so the translator and I spent time sowing in her heart. In the case of the second lady, many times we do not know the outcome of a situation. However, I am reminded that Jesus doesn't promise us an outcome but asks us to be obedient to follow Him always. We have the opportunity to reap a harvest or sow a seed. Both are equally important.

We have the opportunity to be messengers of the hope of the gospel wherever we are geographically. However, what I am learning is that the beauty of global missions highlights the beauty of the gospel: that Jesus came for all colors, cultures and countries. Seeing Him work around the world has expanded my heart and vision, and it has given me a glimpse of what heaven will be like.

## Receiving a Gift
*Patrick Carbary, PA*

Everyone loves to receive a gift. Don't get me wrong, giving gifts is awesome too, but there is something special about opening a present meant just for you. When people receive a gift, they feel thought of, loved and cared for. A gift that can be shared and enjoyed by others separates the good from the great ones. Ephesians 2:8-9 directly speaks to the gift of salvation that God so graciously gives to those who come to faith in Jesus. Paul tells the church of Ephesus, "For by grace you have been saved through faith; and this is not of yourselves, it is the gift of God; not as a result of works, so that no one may boast" (NASB). I've learned that God's indescribable gift of Jesus is not only the greatest gift we can receive, but it is the greatest gift we can share with others.

In April 2019, my wife and I had the privilege of serving on our first healthcare mission trip to Lebanon. Excitement and anticipation filled our hearts as we packed for the Middle East. A team of mostly strangers quickly assembled into a family as we shared stories and collectively asked God to move mightily during our week together. In seemingly no time, lines of expectant patients filled the streets as they awaited their turn to receive care from the clinic. Powerful testimonies began emerging from team members and patients alike. Personally, my favorite encounter of the week took place on what our team later called "Breakthrough Wednesday," thanks to the overwhelming number of personal decisions made by our patients to follow Jesus.

A young Muslim mom and her school-aged daughter were brought to my area in the clinic as the Wednesday afternoon hours carried on. Mom arrived well prepared as she had a stack of reports and various medical records in hand. First, she focused her attention to her daughter, expressing concern over her apparent stunted growth and recent hair loss. I quickly realized my familiar practice of adult emergency medicine had left me in New York. Collectively, we came up with a game plan for her daughter. Mom was relieved and shifted the focus to her concern over her own medical issues. She handed me a stack of papers indicating the issue she came in with was already being treated. Our conversation shifted away from medicine and she began to share some of her life story, which opened the perfect window for me to share the good news of the gospel. I began to unpack God's rescue story and share the gift of Jesus with her through the help of the translator. Occasionally, they would break off and have a two-way conversation in Arabic without my interjection. "Keep going, she's getting it, she's really getting it," the translator exclaimed at one point. I watched the heavy weight of rejection, oppression and heartbreak lift off the mom's shoulders as God's truth came across her ears for the first time. Her countenance and posture visually changed before my eyes. At the end of the conversation, there was not a dry eye amongst the three of us. I remember asking the mom her thoughts on what she had just heard. Her response was one of the most sobering and unforgettable things anyone has ever said to me. "That is so beautiful. I've never heard that before. What do I need to do to have Jesus?" she asked me. She expressed her desire to receive Jesus after a few more minutes of clarification and question asking. I still count the opportunity to pray with her and witness her salvation as my greatest privilege of the week.

The next day, the mom, daughter and other family members returned to the clinic. This time, she had returned specifically to visit and thank me for sharing Jesus with her. The mom gifted me a vase and a bottle of perfume for my wife as a thank you for introducing her to Jesus. This memory always reminds me of the story of Mary in the

Bible. Mary had been touched by Jesus and in return bought the most expensive bottle of perfume, pouring it on His feet. Truly experiencing the love of Jesus creates a deep gratitude inside and creates an understanding of the magnitude of the gift given. Still today, my wife and I keep the vase on our shelf, which reminds us of the power of the gospel and faithfulness of Jesus.

## Waiting Time is Not Wasted Time
*John Pfefferle, DDS*

Perhaps it was becoming "too routine." I have traveled with GHO many times with this mission trip being my sixth GHO team to this location. I knew the drill. Pack, fly over, hope and pray your luggage arrives with you and, if not, return the next day and pick it up. Predictable.

Well, the trip, or should I say "journey," started off with delayed domestic flights, which caused me to miss my international connection, which necessitated a new itinerary. I called to make sure my luggage would be reassigned accordingly, because I was carrying all of the dental supplies necessary for extractions. I called a second time just to make sure and was told my bags were being loaded as we spoke.

Finally arriving at my destination, I discover that none of my three checked bags made it, and I soon learned they never made it out of New York! Clinic was starting the next day, but airlines had no timetable for when my luggage might arrive, which meant seeing extraction patients was impossible. Monday came with no new information on my luggage. So, I decided to go by a dental supply company on Tuesday morning and purchase some basic forceps and miscellaneous supplies. As I was leaving, for some reason, I inquired as to whether they provided repair service, to which they replied, yes, but basically for only one manufacturer, and named the company. Interesting, I thought, because that was the manufacturer that made the portable dental unit the other dentist brought. What a "coincidence."

I finally received my luggage and equipment Wednesday evening, and I was able to get caught up with patients requiring extractions.

But the delay allowed me to spend much more time praying with, talking to, listening and loving on the refugees, which I know was as important, if not more so, than my dental care.

On Thursday morning, I was set up and ready to go! Midway through the day, the other dentist came to inform me that his unit had stopped working. This was a big deal as he was performing necessary fillings and cleanings. That meant those services could not be provided the remainder of the week or all of the next week. Then I remembered my conversation with the dental supply company and that they could service limited equipment, but ours just happened to be what they serviced.

They repaired the equipment and fixed another issue the following week, allowing the dental team to provide all the services we had come to perform, with some buffer time for prayer and just spending time with the refugees while we waited on our equipment.

When I sat back and put it all together, had my luggage not been delayed, I would not have gone to the supply store, and I would not have asked if they serviced equipment, and we would have had a non-functional dental unit. Even as I write this, I can't really explain why I asked about service, as an afterthought I suppose. So, though I waited anxiously, very unhappy with the airlines, I can see there was a purpose to my luggage delay. Wonderful things happened as a result. It reminded me of Romans 8:28, "And we know that God causes all things to work together for good to those who love God, to those who are called according to His purpose" (NASB). Coincidence? Not with God!

# MAURITANIA
## 21.0079° N, 10.9408° W

## The Hands
### Andy Lamb, MD

The hands were heavily stained black, the skin with severe eczematous changes, yet she made no mention of them. She was a young mother who had come to the clinic to have her 6-month-old baby boy seen by the "doctors from America." I was the team leader of our GHO medical team serving in the outskirts of Nouakchott, the capital of Mauritania in Northwest Africa. We were there to provide primary medical care and public health teaching in support of a wonderful Swiss couple who ran a malnutrition clinic for the children of this impoverished country. Mostly, though, we came to love and serve.

Nouakchott is on the edge of the vast Sahara Desert. The people we served had been primarily nomadic, as had their ancestors for centuries before them. They had been forced by an extended drought (who knew a drought could even occur in the Sahara!) to find another way to survive. The physical and emotional needs were as great as I have seen in 20 years of leading medical mission trips internationally.

I examined her baby and reassured her he was healthy. My eyes, though, kept going back to her hands. Finally, I asked to see them. Painful fissures traversed the blackened skin. I asked about her work. She had two jobs, one washing dishes and the other dyeing cloth, and her hands were exposed daily to hours of hot water and caustic irritants. She had no gloves to protect them, no moisturizer to soothe and heal them. She simply did what she had to do to provide for her family.

She was typical of the Islamic women we saw that week. Her face unseen, hidden by her Niqab, a scarf wrapped over the head and covering the face, leaving only the eyes exposed. Her eyes were dark, intense, reflecting an inner strength and determination. I told her how much I respected her for being the strong woman and mother that she was. She sat up straight and looked at me, her eyes "smiling" back. She thanked me and stood to leave. I wondered what would become of her and her baby. Did she have hope that her life would get better? I wanted to believe so. To live without hope is not to truly live.

The majority of people in the world live with no hope of things getting better. Every day is a struggle to survive. Each of you have seen this, too. It may be that patient facing a critical illness, grieving the heartbreak of loss or experiencing the devastation of Alzheimer's. In the busyness of life, may you not miss "the hands" in front of you. May the needs of others become personal to you as they become more real to you. For those of you serving, thank you for seeing a need and going. In doing so, you bring hope, and with hope you bring life, and that makes all the difference.

# MOLDOVA
47.4116° N, 28.3699° E

## Here Am I
*Caroline Adams, RN*

There are so many God sightings from my numerous GHO journeys, it is hard to choose what to share! My first experience on a GHO mission trip was going to Moldova. I had recently had a conversation with the Lord about being too comfortable on past mission trips and how I wanted to get away from just going to be going. I knew He wanted more out of His servant Caroline, but I didn't anticipate this answer. He directed me to the GHO website and the section entitled "Urgent Needs." Moldova immediately came up.

I had never heard of Moldova, but I knew I had to go. I also started to be fearful of the unknown. What if they reject me? What if they are prejudiced? What if I am not competent? I could go on. Doubt is a good strategy of the evil one. My God is a sovereign God, however, and He knows the way He has prepared for us. It turned out this trip changed my life!

I remember standing by the door of the clinic in Moldova on Sunday afternoon. The clinic was to open Monday morning, and we were putting the finishing touches on the triage area. Some of the villagers were walking by curious to see what was going on in this previously abandoned building. A young woman walked by and immediately stopped in front of me. She stared at me and then started to cry. I asked one of the translators to help me communicate with her.

Her name is Tatiana, and as we began talking to her, she started to hug me and touch my face. She told the interpreter she had never seen an African American in person and wanted to touch me. Remember my earlier fear? God used my skin color to open up a door to a gospel conversation! I asked if I could pray with her, and she began telling us her story. She was only 19 years old but was married and had a 2-year-old son. Her son had been removed by the government because she and her husband were heavy drinkers and would not properly take care of the child. She was presently five months pregnant but was so distraught because her son had been taken away from her. She and her husband were of the Roma people, and I learned later they were considered the town alcoholics.

My interpreter and I prayed for her while she wept silently. The weight of her anguish was palpable, and I knew this was a divine appointment. This precious child had never experienced the love of Jesus, but yet He loved her so much He sent a group of people to her to tell her she was loved with an everlasting love. When the prayer finished, she kissed me and asked me to wait where I was. She then went across the street and bought me a box of chocolates and gave them to me. I was broken! She, who had so little, was so willing to give. Thank you, Lord!

We invited her to come to the clinic during the week. Every day I looked anxiously for her, but she never came back. I asked the townspeople for her, but they despised her and her husband and stated she was probably somewhere drinking.

I never saw her again in person, but the Lord has put her before my eyes almost every day since. I have been interceding for her since September 2017. She suffered a miscarriage after a fall and moved away from the village. My prayer for Tatiana is that the Lord would save her, and she would become a mighty evangelist for His name's sake. I believe this with all my heart and pray for her on a weekly basis. I have an assignment from the Lord to stand in the gap for her and intercede. I believe I will see her again—if not on earth, then in heaven.

I will never forget my time in Moldova and the words of Isaiah that says, "Then I heard the voice of the Lord, saying, 'Whom shall I send, and who will go for Us?' Then I said, 'Here am I. Send me!'" (Isaiah 6:8, NASB). I have journeyed with GHO many times since then. And I have many more stories to tell.

## Never!
*Andy Lamb, MD*

"Never! Never have I heard such words come from the mouth of a man!" Her right fist slamming the wooden tabletop. "I want to read that book right now!" She looked at Lloyd as if she suddenly realized something precious had been kept from her.

We were in Moldova, the poorest country in Europe. Once part of the mighty Soviet Union, it was now an independent country struggling to navigate the dramatic upheaval caused by its collapse and the sudden newfound freedom. The road was difficult as 100 years of corruption at every level of government was proving impossible to circumvent. For the Moldovan people, their daily lives had not noticeably changed since the fall of Soviet hegemony. Hopelessness and despair remained, ever present, like a heavy fog on a cold drizzly morning, swallowing them. Communism, democracy, what did it matter? Unemployment rampant; families separated as husbands and wives, mothers and fathers, desperately sought work in neighboring countries, their children left with family or friends; alcoholism epidemic among men, fueled by culture and inflamed by despair and hopelessness; Moldova now the central hub of human trafficking for Europe. It was the "worst hard times." As one Moldovan was heard to say, "The world has either forgotten Moldova or has never heard of it!"

Lloyd and I were the team leaders of our GHO healthcare mission trip. We had led other missions to Moldova and knew the culture and the physical, emotional and spiritual needs that permeated the country. The Russian Orthodox Church and atheism dominated the faith worldview. The concept of a loving, grace-filled, compassionate and accessible God was foreign to them. The priests controlled all matters of faith and more. The Moldovan people live a life where, "The only end to pain is the graveyard," as an elderly, arthritis-crippled woman once said to me as we sat on the steps of her tiny cinder block home, devoid of running water and electricity. She had no hope of anything ever getting better.

On this particular mission trip, team members stay with host families in the village where we serve. This provides a uniquely wonderful opportunity to experience the culture and life of the people we are serving. The interpreters stay with us as well, allowing us to get to know them even better. Our interpreter was Peter, and he proved to be a rich source of cultural and historical knowledge as well as our biggest encourager. Years later, we remain close friends.

The Wednesday night of our week in the village is spent with the host family as we share food, drink and conversation. It is a wonderful time for better understanding the lives they lead and their faith. Our hosts were in their 50s. They were hard working, tough and resilient. Life gave them no other choice. They rarely smiled, and they were atheists. After dinner, we sat in the living room and began asking questions about their lives hoping to gain their trust. For the next two hours, we talked while they sat quietly, listening. Suddenly, to our surprise, the husband began asking the hard questions about God and faith—His existence; good vs. evil; creation vs. evolution; and many more. We answered the ones we could, and when we could not, we spoke of faith. They began to relax and even smile! This gave Lloyd the opportunity to speak on a topic he is passionate about—how men are to love and serve their wives as Christ did the church. While he was talking, the woman, sitting across the table from us, was leaning forward on her forearms, palms flattened against the surface, attentive to every word. Her husband was behind her and to the left, leaning back in his chair, his face without emotion. As Lloyd was finishing, she suddenly lifted her right arm above her head and pounded her fist against the table as she said the words that are forever etched in my mind: "Never! Never have I heard words like this come from the mouth of a man! I want to read that book right now!" Lloyd looked over at her husband and said, "Well, sir, what do you think?" He leaned further back in his chair and after a brief pause said, "It's all right, for now."

As the three of us prepared for bed, we marveled at God's grace and how He is always at work drawing us to Him. It was a reminder of how these healthcare mission trips are about more than providing medical care. They are also about being little "hope-givers," just as Christ is our big "Hope-giver" to a hurting world needing hope. The next day we brought her a Bible in Russian.

## Seeds
### Andy Sanders, MD

For those who have gone on a healthcare mission trip, you know SO much work goes into it. There is seemingly endless preparation for months, including logistical, spiritual, medical, dental, additional healthcare supplies, financial support, etc. And once the team gets to the country, it seems the work is actually just beginning. So much takes place during the trip, so many things are seen and heard, so many feelings are felt, so many thoughts are meditated on. Then we return home, and we might ask ourselves, or others might ask us, if it was worth all of that effort and time. How would we answer that question?

If we were a non-Christian healthcare team, then the question, "Was it worth it?" would have to be answered with various visible metrics, such as how many patients were seen, number of surgeries done, emergencies treated and other such measurable outcomes. One might even look at the numbers of those who professed a new faith in Jesus Christ. Even if benefits are clearly present though, one might personally wonder about the lasting long-term impact of these benefits.

These questions and thoughts are certainly appropriate to have during and after a Christian healthcare ministry trip. However, there is another important, vital part of our team's work that must never be overlooked. It is a small thing that is seldom discussed and is never measured, but we may in fact find out one day in eternity that this one small thing was actually the main thing, the greatest thing, the most valuable and enduring part of our mission trip.

So, the question again: "Was the mission trip worth it?" Before we answer, let me draw our attention to this other small part of our mission trip—seeds.

Seeds are quite small. Besides small, they are unimpressive to look at, and examine them however much you wish, they do not demonstrate any life in them. They bounce when you drop them. They never move when you place them on a table. They are just small, unimpressive, never-changing seeds. Not very exciting. But, as you know, put this seed in soil and add a little water, let it break open, and the change is unimaginable and quite amazing. The seed now grows and becomes something altogether different. And as it matures, it makes more seeds, and the harvest grows and grows and grows over the years and centuries. What a difference between a table-top seed and a planted seed. "Truly, truly I say to you, unless a grain of wheat falls into the earth and dies, it remains alone; but if it dies, it bears much fruit" (John 12:24, NASB).

I was leading a team once to a country in Eastern Europe. We were serving one day in a prison, caring for the young and old men who lived there. It was, as you can imagine, an extremely sobering sight. One of the prisoners who came to see me was a 20-year-old young man who had tried to kill himself by ingesting various materials and cutting himself and soiling his wounds. The guards would not allow him to be transferred out to a hospital. All I could do was simply care for his wounds and give him some oral antibiotics for his severely infected and necrotic wounds. At the end of the visit, I used the Evangecube to share some with him regarding Christ, and I closed in prayer for him. When he left, I found myself struggling with my thoughts. What were we doing there? What were we really accomplishing? This young man came to me so desperate, and there was so little I could do to help him—actually, nothing I could really do for him. I expected he would die in the near future from his infections. I carried an empty feeling within me the next few days.

Then, a year later I returned to that country with a team. One day we returned to that same prison to care for the men there. While there a guard came to tell me that a prisoner wanted to see me, but not as a patient. He just wanted to come and talk. You can imagine my surprise and joy when I saw this young man from a year ago walk into my room. But he wasn't the same man! He was full of joy! And full of health! He said to me, "Do you remember me? I am the young man you saw last year who wanted to die. I swallowed all of those objects and caused the bad skin infections. And do you remember that you told me about Jesus? And when you prayed that prayer, I gave my life to Christ, turning from my sins to my Savior. He has made me all better from my infections. I started a Bible study and there is a group of us now meeting together to study and pray. I have hoped all year that I would see you again to thank you!"

Do you see what I saw now? A seed. A year ago, this seed appeared so lifeless and unimpressive—just a little kindness, a little medical work, a little word from the Bible. But it was a seed! A seed full of divine power to bring about a new life and a multiplying harvest. On this one occasion, the Lord gave me the gift of seeing the early fruits of that seemingly small seed I had planted one year before.

Our healthcare teams, are they worth all the effort, time and cost? We will see many things that will convince us it is indeed worth our labor. But the greatest thing we are doing, the thing of life-changing power, the thing of kingdom-advancing power, the thing of worldwide harvest producing power, is the planting of seeds—seemingly small and unimpressive seeds—but gospel seeds planted into nations, into communities, into churches and into life after life. These seeds are just sitting on the tables of our lives back home, and we now have the privilege on these teams to go and sow them. Some will fall into fertile soil the Lord has prepared. We won't see much of the result, but like with all planted seeds, it is going to yield a great harvest one day. With joy and wonder we can return home and say, "How was our healthcare mission trip? Wow, it was amazing! God called our team, opened a door for our team, sent our team and used our team to sow His seeds!"

## Serving Together
*Kristina Berard, PT, DPT*

My entire experience between applying for the mission trip to Moldova to the plane ride home was a whirlwind and slow motion all at the same time. The Lord had every moment and every step set before me, and all I had to do was step into them.

So here the story begins; I was only a little over two years into practicing physical therapy and was unsure whether I should apply to go on a healthcare mission trip at this point in my career. So, I prayed I would either lose interest or there would be some sort of sign for me to not apply. Well, neither option ever came. I kept getting this nudging feeling to go ahead and apply. At 10:30 p.m. on a Sunday night about seven weeks before the trip, I decided to go ahead and apply and prayed for something to happen with my application if I was not meant to go. To my surprise, I had an email the next morning at 5:07 a.m. welcoming me to serve in Moldova and a list of the things they needed from me. Then the planning began.

I was blessed to get to talk to other physical therapists who had gone to Moldova previously to get an idea of what to expect and what I should bring, from medical supplies to my basic needs. I was a bundle of nerves and excitement with it being the first time I had flown internationally by myself and did not know anyone I would be serving alongside. The flights over there were fine, but the connections were a bit stressful, and it was by the grace of God I made each one. I walked up as they were beginning to board in Chicago when I had been in the airport for roughly three and a half hours!

Finally, I met up with the team I would be serving with! It is amazing how quickly we were able to transition from strangers to friends who felt like we had known each other for years. Jokes and teasing along with deep conversations ebbed and flowed throughout the trip.

I was fortunate that my interpreter was a girl a few years younger than me that I felt able to connect with. In Moldova, the team members are hosted in private homes of church members, so we also had the privilege of living with our interpreters, which helps establish a deeper relationship.

The Lord provided a connection between us that I could have never anticipated or dreamed of having in a few short days. We talked about the basics at first with laughter and moments of warmth drizzled throughout our time serving during the week. But what amazed me was as we were out looking at the stars in the middle of Moldova after a long day, when all of the sudden this sweet young lady began to talk after many moments of silence. To my surprise, she had begun sharing with me things she had struggled with over the last few months. She had suffered through some difficult events previously and had been unable to get them out of her head. I was so touched that she felt comfortable sharing them with me. It was sweet to be able to sit in these moments with her and process them together. The Lord knew just who to send to her and had prepared me through different life events and moments over the last three to five years. It was a gift I could have never expected, known to pray for or even prepare for.

I am forever thankful for those sweet moments we shared that led to a teary eyed and tight gripped moment during our last prayer together, led by our team leader before we said our goodbyes, or better termed, see you later's. Little did she know, she turned a slow burning fire in my heart back into a roaring flame with her vulnerability and longing to honor and serve God and others. Moldova is a place filled with people like this young women living day in and day out to shine for the glory of God. It was my privilege to get to serve alongside of them and to now call many of the men and women on our team not just friends but family.

## Songs of Praise
### Lloyd DeFoor, Non-medical Servant

I loved serving in Moldova and was there on many trips. Moldova trips were different from all of our other trips, because we stayed in people's homes in the villages we served instead of the usual local hotel. Moldova is located between Romania and Ukraine and is one of the former Soviet Union countries. The first time I went I thought it was the darkest and saddest place I had ever seen. Our trips went in late March and April, and it was usually cold and rainy with some snow and sleet mixed in. Most of the homes where we stayed did not have running water or heat. We truly experienced conditions most of the world has every day.

As the years went by, Moldova and the people began to change as they had more freedoms, especially with religion. People's attitudes changed and the countenance on their faces changed. They still lived extremely difficult lives, but they now had hope. When the Soviet Union collapsed, all the capital and financial resources went back to Russia. Jobs in the villages were dried up. Poverty was a tremendous problem. Work was almost impossible to find, and many families were broken as family members had to travel to other countries to find work. Yet still, hope sustains.

We were blessed to serve with some of the brightest, strongest and beautiful people I have ever seen in Moldova. Most of our translators were college students, and we served with some of them many times. They became like our children. The hope they had was not in the government or their jobs but in their personal relationship with Jesus Christ. They loved the Lord, and you could see it on their faces in our worship times. Because we served in some villages that spoke Romanian and some that spoke Russian, we had translators who spoke English, Romanian and Russian. Some of them spoke several more languages. These were bright young people. I have a hard time speaking English!

I think the closest I have ever felt to God was in a home in Moldova. We ate in people's homes and all of us ate together. One late afternoon we were waiting on dinner to be served and we were sitting around singing. They, not me, would sing a verse in Romanian, then sing it in Russian and then sing it in English. I spent my time looking in the faces of those beautiful young people and the joy they were feeling as they were worshiping the Lord through song. I think I got a glimpse of what heaven is going to look like. I only hope that one day I might have the faith incredible group of young showed through their hope in Jesus. We do serve an awesome God!

# MONGOLIA
46.8625° N, 103.8467° E

## Forsaking Buddha
*Phillip L. Aday, DDS*

Our GHO team had finally arrived at our ministry site in inner Mongolia after a 30-hour train ride through China and a really long flight to China. Exhaustion doesn't describe it well enough. Once we had some rest, we set about planning for our clinic.

Our team had been given an entire wing of a new hospital to see patients. We were partnering with a couple of national doctors, and our host was providing translators. We were warned that we needed to be cautious about openly sharing the gospel with our patients, since there was a strong possibility some of our patients might be government officials who would report us.

I was treating dental patients who needed fillings and cleanings. Our patients were a mix of nationals who spoke Chinese or Mongolian, so our translators were necessary for us to communicate with our patients,

I had given my patient, Xi, an injection to numb the area I was going to be treating. While we were waiting for the local anesthetic to take effect, I looked over at the translator, Mary, to see if she thought it was okay to share the gospel with our patient. She gave me a nod indicating it was okay. I shared the gospel with Xi using short phrases since Mary was having to translate my words into Chinese. After Mary had finished translating, Xi pulled out a small Jade Buddha from around her neck and stated, "This is what I worship."

On all my mission trip encounters, I have felt strongly that unless the Holy Spirit speaks to an individual leading them to accept Him as their Lord and Savior, I should not attempt to pressure anyone to decide to become a Christ follower. In my opinion, a coerced decision has the strong possibility of being less than genuine.

After Xi indicated she worshiped Buddha, I felt she would not be receptive to any further discussion about Christ. I sat back to wait for the local anesthetic to take effect. While I was waiting, Mary continued to speak with Xi. After a couple of minutes, Mary spoke to me in English and stated Xi was willing to include Jesus, along with her continued worship of Buddha. As gently as I could, I explained that adding Jesus to her continued worship of Buddha would not be acceptable to Jesus. Again, I sat back, still not feeling the Holy Spirit leading me to share any further with her. Mary continued to speak with Xi, and in a few minutes, Mary indicated Xi was willing to accept Jesus as her Savior and worship Him only! I have to admit at this point I felt Mary, while well intentioned, might have badgered Xi into saying "yes" to the gospel to please us. I was also aware the Holy Spirit works in ways we cannot know.

Through Mary's interpretation, I led Xi through a prayer of confession and accepting Jesus as her personal Savior. To my surprise and joy, my doubts vanished. As Xi said, "Amen," she reached up and took off the necklace with the jade Buddha and asked, "Now what do I do with this?" Having committed her life to Jesus Christ, she was now willing to forsake her idol worship of Buddha. Wow! I was blown away and was so thankful Mary had persisted in gently leading Xi to a point of decision.

"Now what do I do with this?" Xi's question still needed an answer. I told Xi she could destroy it, signifying her decision to not worship Buddha now that she had accepted Jesus Christ. Or, if she would allow me, I would take the jade Buddha back to the United States with me and share the story of how she had rejected Buddha and become a Christ-follower. Xi placed the small idol in my hand. I still have that small jade Buddha and have shared Xi's story of redemption with my local church and other believers. I occasionally take out that small figure of Buddha and wonder how Xi is doing in her walk with the

Lord. It also serves as a reminder that without Mary's perseverance in engaging Xi in her heart language, I would have passed up this wonderful privilege of leading Xi to faith in Christ. And it's a reminder to pray for her. What a privilege it is, to intervene for those we have connected with over the years on the mission field and place them at the very throne of His grace.

# NICARAGUA
## 12.8654° N, 85.2072° W

## Can God Use Me?
### *Jackie Michik, Non-medical Servant*

I was asked by someone at my church to consider serving on a health-care mission trip to Nicaragua with GHO. This was a venue of service I thought I had lost long ago. Toward the end of college and for a bit after that I worked as an EMT/firefighter on Milwaukee's streets and in surrounding rural areas as well as in the emergency room. I have seen a lot. Working as an emergency medicine physician is what I hoped and dreamed to do with my life.

I was well on my way and in my first year of medical school when a car accident landed me in the emergency room as a patient. I had a hand injury that developed into a critical condition called compartment syndrome. This is when the swelling from an injury or an infection increases the pressure inside so much that the area starts to lose blood flow and the tissue begins to die. Limb threatening! I almost did lose my right hand, and I am right-handed. I ended up with residual hand weakness and loss of function with limitations that ended my hopes for a medical career. I also developed a chronic severe hand pain due to a condition called Reflex Sympathetic Dystrophy. It took multiple doctor visits, surgeries and procedures over the next few years to save my hand and achieve reasonable pain management. As you can imagine, depression ensued after losing my chance to complete medical school and fulfill the dream I believed God had called me to. Where does a true medical-minded believer in Jesus Christ go after that? I had no idea, but I thought I was done. There would be no chance to serve God through medicine.

Thankfully, years later I came across an awesome brother in Christ who put a bug in my ear, and graciously a foot to my rear, about serving on a healthcare mission team. Sometimes, that is what we desperately need! We're not done until we're in the ground. Whatever one's background might be, the book is not closed while you are here on this earth. There is work to be done.

I could barely eat a bite in the couple of months prior to my first mission trip. The anxiety threatened to paralyze me. In my head, the idea that I might possibly still be useful for the kingdom was way beyond my ability to grasp. And honestly, I was afraid of what our Holy God was ready to do in me. But for some reason (thank you, Good Lord), I pressed on. Never in my entire life have I felt more like I was doing what God intended than on the mission field.

I served in several different roles while on our mission trip. I was able to work at triage and do the initial assessment of patients and check vital signs. This allowed me to meet many of the people we were serving. I will never forget the first lady who broke my heart. She had a chronic wound to her foot, yet she stood in line for at least three hours to be seen. She will never have access to the type of medical care and equipment I had that saved me from losing my hand, a treatment that reintroduced me to productive life. After cleaning and redressing her wound and teaching her how to use a walker we were able to give her, my translator and I cried and prayed with her. I had to take a break to cry and pray alone with my God who loves me. And her. It was a powerful moment of spiritual healing.

I was blessed to serve in the role of public health education servant on my second mission trip. I have the technical, biological and medical background to understand and teach this. GHO does an expanded patient assessment, including teaching how to take vital signs and treat dehydration among other first aid treatments to our local national partner servants. They will then use this training to help their community and continue to educate others. God gave me a venue to serve using the gifts and knowledge He has given me along with using my gift of compassionately connecting with people as I present information.

I love Nicaragua. My very first GHO trip involved resting within hearing of gunshots. This is not usual for a mission trip, but we were serving in Nicaragua just as protesting was beginning from people angry at government authorities. It did not matter! I've got amazing brothers and sisters who I wouldn't know apart from this mission opportunity. True servant-hearted believers are tough to find these days. GHO gave me a chance to serve, and I took it! We have an amazing God standing behind and before us! I would encourage anyone to step out and serve in His name. You will be amazed what God can do in and through you!

## Cast Out Demons
### Ron Brown
### Associate Director, GHO

My wife Becky and I, along with the GHO team, had driven some five hours up into the mountains near the border with Honduras, to the town of San Juan de Rio Coco, Nicaragua. Our own children's pastor from our local church, Tony, was on his first mission trip with us, and he had a great experience providing a children's program. His setting was the front porch of a poor woman's home on the edge of our clinic site, where this postage stamp size area hosted 30 to 40 kids at any given time during that week. The woman was usually on the porch ready to help when she wasn't cooking on an open fire or nursing her baby, right there in front of Tony, which, of course, is the most normal thing in the world for most cultures and countries. One highlight was when he had the kids coloring Bible stories, and the local policemen who were sent to provide security for the clinic asked if they could color as well. Like many adults around the developing world, they likely had never colored anything before in their lives.

Wednesday evening while we were eating supper, a knock came on the door of our meeting/dining room. Some of the team and interpreters tried to attend to the young teenage girl, Cherith, as she was asking if we had a psychiatrist on our team. I was asked to talk to her and found out a bit more of her story, and I invited her to come to the clinic the next day during our lunch hour so we could give her a lengthy focused time.

So Cherith promptly returned the next day at noon, and Becky and I, along with another female interpreter, took her to the nearby hotel patio, where our interpreters were being lodged. She was wearing these woolen black gloves with skull designs all over them. She wore jeans and a black top and had a chain attached to something in her jeans pocket. We grabbed some chairs and asked her to tell us her story, after finding a shady spot to sit. The salient points included the fact that her father was a Satan worshiper and had given her over to Satan upon his death.

As she began to open up, she asked us to take down the mirror that was on the outside wall of the patio bathroom, as she said her dad often communicated with her through any mirror, though he was now dead some years ago. So, we turned the mirror over and she shared many disturbing details of a childhood that was full of evil influences, manifestations and horror. She heard voices and was being driven mad by all these experiences past and present. She wanted to know what we could do for her.

We explained that Jesus was the only answer for her torment and that He alone offered her salvation from her sins and past. He could cast out the demons that haunted her. She agreed to commit her life to Christ and receive forgiveness and freedom. We asked her if she wanted to get rid of her gloves, but she could not get them to come off.

Our interpreter was led to have her read Romans 10:9-10, "...if you confess with your mouth the Lord Jesus and believe in your heart that God has raised Him from the dead, you will be saved. For with the heart one believes unto righteousness, and with the mouth confession is made unto salvation" (NKJV).

So, we showed her the verses and asked her to repeat them to lead her into salvation. She read the first words but could not repeat, "Lord

Jesus," and she began to manifest, as she was demonized. Contortions, cursing and flailing began, and we responded by singing hymns about the blood of Jesus, invoking the power of the name of Jesus and quoting Scriptures. This went on for some 20 to 30 minutes. The demons were losing their hold on her, and she continued to try and read those two verses.

Finally, after many attempts, she was able to read the entire passage. She then took the Bible we were using and embraced it to her chest as she wept and rejoiced over being saved and delivered. We queried her to see if there remained any false or deceptive spirits. Something we learned from our years serving with Native Americans in Arizona, without Cherith realizing it, was to place the Bible on her back, while Becky was talking to her. She never reacted to the Bible touching her, so we knew she was totally free, as demons hate the Word of God.

We asked her if she wanted to get rid of her gloves and she smiled and easily removed them. Then she said she had some things in her pocket and on her chain that she wanted to get rid of. We asked her if we could have a celebration ceremony, and we called Tony and other team members who had been praying for us during our session with her.

We started a little fire, and she threw her gloves and objects into the flames as we began singing hymns and songs of victory. It was one of those special moments when you could almost hear angels joining us, celebrating over a sinner who now has her name written in the Lamb's book of life and is free from sin, demons and daily torment. What a glorious experience it was for all of us to see the power of God's Word, the power of the blood and name of Jesus. To watch before our eyes the transformation, healing and deliverance by the power of Jesus Christ. "So if the Son sets you free, you will be free indeed" (John 8:36, ESV).

One of our local support pastors for the GHO clinic agreed to take in Cherith, who was gifted in children's work and babysitting. So, for the next weeks she became part of their family and experienced love, care and discipleship like never before in her life. Our interpreter kept up with her over the next months and years.

Cherith means to "cut off or cut down" in Hebrew. We saw first-hand that she cut down the evil that her dad had imposed on her and cut off the demonic ties as she embraced the King of Kings and Lord of Lords.

## Every Opportunity
*Andrew Shock, PA*

We were serving in the mountains of Nicaragua, near San Juan Del Rio Coco. As happens often on our mission trips, we had a 20- to 30-minute bus ride to and from our hotel and clinic site every morning. Our clinic was temporarily set up at a community school in the area we were serving. Midway between the hotel and clinic was a section of road under construction. There was a crew of about 10 workers every morning and evening as we drove by. We would wave to them every time we drove past them. They enjoyed our brief encounters and always waved back with gusto!

On our Tuesday evening drive back to our hotel, we stopped to visit with them for a short while and I gave each of them a Bible tract written in Spanish. I started praying that someone would be able to share the gospel with them and to help them understand what they were reading and answer any questions they may have.

Two days later, after continuing to wave and greet each other on the daily drives, I was out conducting home visits with a small GHO team when we stopped for refreshments at a small store on the same road. It was on a banana and coffee plantation. The woman who ran the store asked me to come into her house and see her parents for medical issues. As we were visiting with the store owners, the road crew stopped at the home for lunch. The store owner brought them into her own personal dining room and cooked for them in her own personal kitchen. So, while they were seated and waiting to be served, I went in and asked them, with the help of my interpreter, what they thought of the tracts. It led to an opportunity to use the Evangecube and share the gospel with all of them. Several store workers and people who lived in the home were there as well. They were a very attentive group and were interactive, asking questions and responding to questions.

I am thankful for all those who put in the effort to develop tracts and tools like the Evangecube that help us share the gospel across cultures and language barriers. I was grateful the Lord heard my previous prayer and opened the door to this time of sharing. You never know what might happen! Being obedient. Going as He has commanded, to go and preach the gospel to all creation. He blesses us as we try to bless others.

## The Eyes of Jesus
*Trish Burgess, MD*
*Director, Global Health Outreach*

I was serving with GHO on my very first mission trip ever. I had other opportunities, but I never felt led to go just because my church or someone else was going somewhere. I wanted it to be between me and the Lord. Go somewhere with Jesus because He alone said so. I waited, and I learned a whole lot before He finally said, "Okay, now you can go." It was almost another year before I signed on to a mission team and went. His timing is perfect.

My husband dropped me off at the airport and I went with a lump in my throat, a little unsure as I left him and my three children behind. I just knew I had to be obedient. It wasn't easy though. So, Jesus and I flew to Nicaragua to join a team of 40 or so, none of whom I knew. What a beautiful place and people to meet for a first-time mission trip! My heart was ready to work hard and serve with all my might.

As my very first day of clinic was winding down, I was tired. I certainly had gotten my wish to work hard! The interpreter had wandered off since we had no more patients waiting when the triage nurse began helping a mom walk her daughter back to see me. They were actually practically dragging her daughter since she couldn't walk. They each had an arm around her. I could see clearly that she was special needs. I said in a whispered breath, "What am I going to do for her?" and "I have nothing to offer her!" So, I tried to get out of it. I explained to the nurse that I didn't have an interpreter but pointed to a nearby physician who did. She plopped that child and mom in my chairs and said, "I'll get you one!" She told me later God told her to bring her to me. And I, in my weakened flesh, tried to get rid of her! Get rid of one who turned out to be one of the greatest blessings that ever happened to me! Oh, how my heart and flesh may fail!

So, with a new interpreter I began to talk with her momma. Her daughter's name was Glennis, and she was clean and smelled powdery fresh and was obviously well cared for. Her husband had abandoned her and her daughter. She had been born healthy but contracted meningitis at six months old, resulting in severe brain damage. She could not walk or talk, see other than some light and shapes and had seizures. Her mom made and sold pastries at bus stops to afford her seizure medicine. She had two questions for me. One, could I (as an American doctor) heal her? And two, if she somehow managed to get her to the United States of America, could they heal her there? I began to talk to her about brain damage and how it was permanent and there would be no physical cure for her daughter. I did reassure her that she was obviously taking really good care of her. I had learned long ago that sometimes who your patient is, is not who you think it is. In this case, her momma was my patient. She needed to learn that she was doing all she could for her daughter, and all without the additional resources, wheelchair, physical therapy, etc. that would be available back home in the U.S. I did ask the national doctor working with our clinic to talk with mom, to make sure she was connected with any resources that may be available to her.

While the doctor was talking to her momma, Glennis kept looking my direction with her unfocused gaze and leaning toward me. So, I scooped her on to my lap and began rocking her and singing softly, "Jesus loves me, this I know...." She would tuck her face into my neck and just hug me. She would occasionally lean back a bit and look toward me with her unfocused gaze with a huge smile. It was a moment in His presence. The Scriptures say, "What you do for them, to the least of these, you do for me" (Matthew 25:40, paraphrase). I realized I was holding Jesus Christ Himself in my arms and loving Him through this beautiful, precious broken vessel. I felt Him. A crowd began to notice. A violinist on the team came over and began to play the music to go along with my song. (I know, right? There was a violinist on the team?) It was one of the most beautiful, tender moments in my walk with the Lord.

When the Nicaraguan doctor and momma finished their conversation, she took her child back in her arms. I was overwhelmed. But then, Glennis looked back at me and suddenly her eyes changed. They went from her unfocused gaze and were transformed into the eyes of Jesus Christ Himself. For just a couple of seconds they were focused and looking directly into mine. They showed warmth, wisdom and a touch of humor. Through that two-second gaze, Jesus was asking me, "Aren't you glad you came?" Oh yes, Lord. Yes, I am! It was a calling. It was a commissioning of sorts for me. I knew GHO was my ministry. I knew why I had been created, to do these missions for the Lord. He had plans for my life that were finally revealed. I will never forget it or "the look!"

## God Directs the Director
*Rolando Castillo*
*GHO Nicaragua Director*

I serve as the GHO Nicaragua Director and have been blessed to plan and prepare for many GHO teams over the years. I have also developed relationships with pastors all over my country who do their best to assist our teams. We pray for God to guide us to where the next GHO team should serve. We had the opportunity to work in the mountains in the northern part of Nicaragua. We worked in a small and very remote community called Quibuto. We had no doubt the Holy Spirit was the one who sent us to this place, even when it was very hard to get a permit to use the local primary school building for our medical team to serve these poor communities. We thank God for the entire team doing such an outstanding job throughout the week providing medical and dental care for these needy people.

Sometimes, we are able to add a pastor training conference on to the work of a GHO team. The pastoral conference was a blessing to more than 20 pastors from different denominations who diligently attended the meetings. Some of the team members had the privilege to teach and share with these servants from the Lord more about discipleship and its importance. The pastors were challenged to work on their vision and strategy for their churches in order to be more effective for the expansion of the kingdom of God. At the end of the course, they were able to receive a discipleship book and study Bible. We need to keep praying that the impact of God's Word will be a blessing for many families in these mountains through these faithful pastors.

During a week of work on the mission field we have the chance to see how the Lord is changing lives. Many of our patients, and even sometimes volunteers helping to serve with us, are convicted by the Holy Spirit to recommit their lives to Him. There was a young lady, Mary, who felt convicted of her own brokenness as she was leading a young girl to accept Jesus for the first time. At that time, she knew she couldn't continue on with her broken relationship she had with the Lord. In that moment of understanding, Mary decided to restore that relationship. God not only worked in the hearts of the people we helped, but He also worked in the lives of many team members. Glory to His wonderful name! We need to remember to keep praying for our patients, and we also need to keep praying for our team members. It is a privilege to serve God through GHO and watch Him work in the lives of our people.

## God is Real
### Brittany Hnida, Non-medical Servant

Our team returned from Nicaragua months ago, and I thought as soon as I returned I would know what to say to update my family and friends who supported our team through prayers, money and well wishes. Thinking through this is a part of a mission trip and can be difficult as we experience re-entry. The culture shock of re-entry is often worse than the original culture shock of arriving in a foreign country!

Unfortunately, I was hit with the worst case of writer's block, and I could not figure out how to best summarize my experience for those who were not there in Nicaragua with us. Now, almost five months after our return, I am still processing what we experienced for that short week. I know that no matter what I say, nothing will be an adequate reflection of how our time was spent.

All I can say is that the God I have been taught about since I was a small child became real to me in ways I have never experienced before. I saw Him in the faces of the people we served, in their smiles and in their eyes. I heard Him in the laughter of the children when they reunited with a team member who has known them since they were a baby. I felt Him moving with our team as we reached through the darkest evil to share the light of Christ with those who had never heard His name before. I experienced His love in an indescribable way that I cannot help but to share with anyone who asks. And I pray I reflect that in every aspect of my life.

I hope to return to Nicaragua again in the future. I am already asking friends and family to please be in prayer for our teams as we work to return and for those we will hopefully be ministering to once again in Nicaragua. Taking that first step of faith and joining a mission trip is huge! But God teaches you, grows you, speaks to you through your service in His name. I pray to be the hands and feet of Jesus each time I go, and I always end up seeing Him in the very people I am there to help. What a blessing!

## God Meets Our Needs
*Jeremy Hutton, PT*

I had the opportunity to learn about GHO through a team leader, Dr. Griff, who is a dentist who led a prayer group I was in at Lincolnton Methodist Church. It was inspiring to learn how they served by offering free healthcare to the needy as a means to offer a spiritual healing as well by sharing the gospel message. I did not realize they needed allied health professionals and non-medical volunteer servants to help with their teams. I was encouraged to come on a GHO mission trip with him. I thought the trips were for physicians and dentists, but he told me physical therapists like myself were very useful, so I signed up to go with him on a trip to Nicaragua.

I got a call from one of the GHO physical therapy consultants, who told me bringing durable medical equipment like wheelchairs, walkers, canes, etc. was my job, and that wheelchairs were a "life changer" for disabled folks in third world countries. "How many should I bring?" was my main question, and he said that every situation was different and there was no way of knowing, but that I should pray about it, which I did.

We were high in the mountains in northern Nicaragua for that mission trip, and I had brought six wheelchairs donated by the retirement community in Savannah Lakes South Carolina, where I worked. By the end of the week, exactly six Nicaraguan patients needed wheelchairs! To be honest, things didn't always work out so neatly on other trips, and I have had too few at times. On my most recent trip I had too many. On my last trip, also in the beautiful Nicaraguan mountains, I had three wheelchairs left over. Fortunately, a Nicaraguan physician whose father was a pastor and who grew up in the area told me she could find homes for them and promised to send me pictures of the people who received them. A month later I received those pictures, along with one showing wheelchairs strapped to either side of a donkey, the only way to deliver them to the disabled who live in extremely remote areas.

Sometimes the Lord provides perfectly just what we need. Sometimes we don't have enough, which can feel heartbreaking and very humbling. I try to remember in those moments that we are not the only means for the Lord to provide, and we can pray for Him to meet the needs that we cannot. Sometimes He provides an overabundance. It is then that I realize I don't need to see everything to the end. I can trust that His provision is always perfect, and it may sit waiting for someone we don't even know about. And that's okay. I don't need to see His tapestry completed to appreciate how beautifully He can weave the thread of my life into others as He joins our stories to His.

## Holy Spirit Speak Quick!
### Craig Amnott, MD
### Harold Boro, Non-medical Servant

Craig was leading a GHO mission trip in Nicaragua, and we had a small team of four or five of our regular trip participants doing home visits. These small teams leave the rest of the team running the regular clinic and do home visits to those who are home bound and not able to come to our clinic. We were just finishing up our third or fourth home visit and were running behind schedule.

While the doctors were inside taking care of the family in this home, more and more people started to gather outside as word went through the neighborhood we were there. People were bringing their sick in hopes of seeing the doctor. Harold and other team members were staying outside trying to get the sick people inside to see the doctors. We had another planned stop, but due to the rush of people, the doctors decided to stay put. Well, people just kept coming and coming. By the time the doctors packed up, we were way behind schedule. Not everyone had a chance to see the doctors, so we were communicating as best we could with the little Spanish we knew that they should come to our clinic. When Craig came out of the house, he was behind schedule, which does not happen often!

Harold felt the Holy Spirit telling him we could not leave without sharing the gospel to everyone. Harold said, "Craig, I can feel the Spirit telling me that we have to stay here a bit longer." Craig was hot, tired, rain soaked and running low on patience, so he blurted back to Harold, "Harold! The Spirit is not talking to you right now, and we are running behind schedule. Let's get going!" Harold, who by nature is very easy going and a natural people person, reared back and basically told Craig that no matter what he said, we were going to stay put for a few more minutes. At that moment, Craig heard the Spirit within him say (his word's, not the Spirit's words), "Shut up, Craig, listen to Harold and stop worrying about your schedule! I've got this." Craig pouted something back to Harold to the nature of, "Okay, we'll stay a few more minutes but I better see the Spirit move pretty quick!"

So, we gathered the large group outside, and Harold shared the gospel story. At the end, he gave the group the opportunity for anyone there who wanted to receive the love of Christ into their heart and begin their walk with Jesus. There was silence in the crowd, no one answered. Just maybe, this time was for the planting of the seed of Christ. We waited a little longer. At this point, Craig was ready to pick Harold up and throw him in the back of the pick-up truck! He asked for another minute because he sensed the Spirit at work. The Spirit was doing a work on Craig also, because he said, "Yes, go ahead."

Over the next five minutes, Craig stood back in awe as Harold proceeded to share a little more about the gospel to this small group of Nicaraguans. It wasn't long before one of the women, "the woman at the well" according to those who knew her as a woman of loose morals, accepted Jesus as her Lord and Savior! She began to cry and said, "Yes, me." Harold led her in a prayer of salvation. God is so faithful!

How many times do we deny ourselves a blessing because we are in too much of a hurry to discern the Spirit speaking to us? You can't make this stuff up! You can only choose to experience it yourself by joining us on a mission trip!

## I Believe!
### Sue Boro, Non-Medical Servant

On my second or third GHO trip, I was assigned to go on home visits to a remote place in Nicaragua. We went to a hut where a young family lived because the father was ill. I remember chickens running in and out, and there were quite a few young children. Dr. Craig examined and spoke with the man as we listened. The man had been to a doctor about this ailment a few months prior and showed Craig his paper from that visit. His wife looked scared. Craig told us the man was dying, that his organ systems were actually shutting down.

Craig asked the man if he had faith in God. The man explained that he'd heard about God and that Jesus was the Savior, but he didn't have a faith of his own. Craig then went on to make sure the guy understood that we are eternal beings, and after we die, we go on to be with God in heaven or be tormented forever in hell. And in classic Dr. Craig style he said, "You're really close to heading into one of those two places. What's your choice?"

As great as that event is in itself, for the man chose Life, what happened on the periphery of that is what most impacted me. After hearing of the father's impending future, I approached his young wife and in my best Spanish (which was so awful I made my teammates giggle), I told her the gospel. An interpreter at one point joined and helped out. I also promised her that somehow, some way God would provide for her if she would believe and follow Him.

As I spoke these words, I was struck by the audaciousness of what I was saying. And for the rest of that day and on into the night, it played over and over in my head and heart because God opened a window for me to realize that I meant those words. I said them because I really believed it. The whole Jesus is the Savior thing. I believed it! I could not, with any good conscience, have pleaded with her to believe in the way of hope unless I thought it was true. And I did. That in itself, the gift of belief, is from God. I do! I cry even writing this because it bolsters my faith and gratitude yet again to remember and think on it.

# Iron Sharpening Iron
*Ron Brown*
*Associate Director, Global Health Outreach*

I began working at GHO full-time as the Associate Director in 1999. I have been greatly blessed to be part of more than 80 GHO teams in some 25 countries on five continents. It has been an honor to serve with the "crem de la crem" from CMDA members on these GHO teams, as well as amazing national partners and interpreters. Team leaders have been forged from these teams and have become my dearest of friends as elements of iron sharping iron. Among my favorite teams have been ones that served in prisons, where I also met many godly men and women serving behind bars.

From the first year in 1999 serving with Dr. Sam Molind, our first GHO Director, I learned so much and was amazed how God used him to basically start everything from scratch, including our GHO team manuals, site visit forms, patient forms and affiliations with countries and universities, plus acquiring surgical, dental and medical equipment and the medicines to fill our unique formularies. He did all our initial site visits and, in time, used our team leaders to help decide which countries to launch our next GHO teams. We went from 10 teams to 20 and then 30 and 40 a year.

Dr. Don Thompson was passed the GHO Director baton for seven years and solidified our department, improved processes, managed inventory and expanded GHO into more countries and volunteers to the peak of having more than 1,100 GHO participants a year into over 45 countries.

In 2018, Dr. Trish Burgess became our director and used her experience as an emergency room doctor of 20 years and serving on many GHO teams and then leading teams. Her focus is to raise our standards on patient care and safety, greatly improving our community education and focus on training national lay folks to carry on basic care with skills to help patients monitor blood pressures, wound and burn care and treat dehydration, as well as greatly improving our continuing education offerings before or after the actual team trip. God used circumstances to help us open up new fields of ministry, especially in limited-access countries, to reach unreached people groups in an even greater way the last three years.

It has been a great joy to be the Associate Director and serve each one of these chosen and gifted GHO directors. By default, I became the GHO historian the last 22 years, maintained relationships with national partners and learned lessons that have better prepared us for opening new fields to reach even more of the least, the lost and the last.

As a layman serving as a team leader, I found a wonderful area in the reading glass clinic that brought me such joy. I have received countless smiles, hugs and even tears when an elderly person is able to read their Bible again after years of not being able to, or even thread a needle or do manual craftwork. We have trained countless laypeople to work in our reading glass clinic and even help detect cataracts or pterygium. Other servants have learned to work in the dental clinic to clean dental instruments, hold a flashlight or hold a fearful child's hand. Counting pills in the pharmacy and helping bag, organize and work with pharmacists to hand out medicines are all extremely valuable roles for our servants, who truly are the hands and feet of Jesus.

While serving on a Nicaragua mission trip, I remember how God would bring me just the right person in the reading glass line that was ready to receive Christ. So, I would see maybe 10 to 15 patients, get them glasses and pray for them for a total of five minutes. Then, someone would sit in the patient chair and God would nudge me and say this one is ready. That happened about five times that day, where a low hanging fruit was just waiting to hear the gospel message so they could surrender their lives and become a new believer in Christ. When we pray for God to draw people and then to convict them, our part is simply to share the gospel message and the claims of Christ. It is amazing how simple it is to point hungry souls to the Savior, who alone knows how to satisfy them, nourish them and give them eternal and abundant life.

Another impactful part of our teams is our evening devotions. I was preparing to give a devotion but could not for the life of me determine what God wanted me to speak about. As it came time for our evening sharing time, I felt like I literally went to the front of the room, where we held our team evening devotions, and opened my mouth and God filled it. I began to talk about a GHO team that Dr. Molind led to China and some of the amazing things that happened and how a handful of folks came to faith in Christ. When I finished sharing that evening, a young doctor came up to thank me for speaking about China. He and his wife and kids later were called and served in China. He shared with me that God had told him I was going to share about China and it would be significant to him and his future. That truly amazed me, as I had no idea what I was going to talk about until I literally opened my mouth and God put the China story in my heart and mouth.

It is an amazing experience to feel that God used you to further His kingdom. Not by any special gift or talent that we may have, but simply by our willingness to be obedient. I have been blessed to serve with GHO for so many years!

## Machete Miracle
*Rhonda Wright, NP*

"Lord, give me a clear mind, steady hands and a big heart." This is a prayer I have prayed thousands of times over my career. As a former paramedic, emergency, flight and critical care nurse and currently practicing critical care nurse practitioner, I have spent my career in highly stressful, often remote and intense situations. I had no idea why God gave me such a restless heart and pushed me to press on to advance my career into various avenues, never being content where I was. Finally, after 42 years, He showed me why.

Serving in Nicaragua, it was a typical afternoon clinic when, suddenly, a young girl named Mireyda was carried in with an abdominal evisceration. I would later learn that she and her brother were riding their horse and carrying a machete, when the horse bucked and somehow the machete penetrated her abdomen causing a complete evisceration and what appeared to be bowel damage. We all immediately went to work assessing the situation and grabbing for supplies. Mireyda was alert but sluggish. We "happened to have" decent trauma dressings and were able to cover the wound and control the bleeding. We found large bore IVs and were able to rapidly place two and start fluids. Knowing our formulary, I was aware that we did not have the best antibiotics for such a wound but "somehow," in another box of supplies, I found one bottle of cefazolin and got this going in addition to the formulary ceftriaxone. It is amazing how many times God provides just what we need.

Our Nicaraguan physician partners were there helping as well. Despite our language barriers, we communicated. What was becoming keenly unclear was, where do we go from here? I was then told that an ambulance was coming from an hour away and a pediatric surgeon was in the little town of Siuna, where our team had been staying. I was told, "You're going with her." We loaded her into a pickup truck and I and my interpreter, Roy, went with her.

On the way our patient started looking a bit grey. Roy suggested, "You better pray with her in case she doesn't make it!" I prayed a prayer myself because I did not know what to say. But through my interpreter, I started telling her about Jesus while holding her hand. I knew she heard the voice of God through us. We met the ambulance and helped transfer her.

I have no idea how often a pediatric surgeon serves in this tiny community. I would love to know if they "just happened" to be there that day. The next day, we were able to hear that her surgery went well, and within a couple of days she was up, walking around and taking clear liquids. By the grace and provisions of God, she is now home and healed!

Someone said to me, "Now you know what all those years of training and changes and experiences were for!" Halfway joking, I said, "I'm so glad I finally know!" Then it hit me. God's perfect plan and timing. There would have been no clinic in that remote village had we not been obedient. There would have been no lifesaving intervention for Mireyda. There would have been no sharing of Jesus. The clarity of my life's testimony and purpose was never more real—obedience to the call! I was born to meet people where they are. I was born to go make disciples! My medical skills and training are tools I was given to meet people in the worst of situations, whether in tragedies, or extreme temperatures, or in prison, or without clean water or among the threat of diseases or corrupt governments. I have been called to the mission field in a mighty way, and I praise God for those skills and training that give me an avenue to bring His love and healing to the remote corners of a hurting world! I can be silent no longer! I must be obedient to the Great Commission. Not one of us will fall without His knowledge! And look at what He did to save one!

## Miracle Shoes
### *Trish Burgess, MD*
### *Director, Global Health Outreach*

I was serving on a mission team to Nicaragua and brought my entire family along to serve together, including my husband and three children. We were working on Ometepe Island, Nicaragua, and the team leader requested we bring shoes to donate since they were hard to get on the island. We lived near the University of Georgia and the athletic director donated lots of tennis shoes from the athletes. Apparently at the end of each sports season, they turn in the barely worn game shoes. We had way more shoes donated than we were able to bring, but each of my five family members carried one suitcase full of shoes. (We left all the size 14 and above!) We also brought a few pairs of smaller shoes that we donated from my children's personal closets. One of them was a pair of lime green converse tennis shoes.

My family enjoyed serving immensely. My engineer husband worked in the eyeglass clinic and my three children, ages 11, 13 and 16 at the time, rotated through several areas of the clinic. My daughter, Marisa, worked at triage the first couple of days helping to escort patients where they needed to go from triage. On the second day of clinic, we were already running out of shoes! She helped assist an elderly lady who had trouble walking from triage to the medical waiting area. The lady asked Marisa about shoes, and she said she would check but they were running low. So, Marisa went to check while her patient waited in line.

Marisa did indeed find that a few pairs of shoes were left, but only one pair was available in this lady's size. You guessed it, her lime green converse! So, she brought them back for the lady to try on. She was wearing a pale pink dress and you can just imagine how they looked! When Marisa went to help her when it was her turn to be seen by the doctor, the lady told her she didn't need to help her. She could walk! It turned out she was having trouble walking because her shoes were way too small and her toes were curling under, making her balance difficult. Marisa came running to find me in the clinic to get my camera so she could get her picture and share her story! She was so excited to have helped!

At the team closing just a few days later, Marisa had this to say; "What I learned is you can give anything to God, even a used pair of shoes, and He can make a miracle with it!"

Who would not want their child to learn this lesson? Oh, the faith of children! How precious in His (and their momma's) sight!

## Porch Visit
### Harold Boro, Non-medical Servant

I was serving on a small part of our team doing home visits to strategic areas or persons that our in-country church partners were aware needed a home visit. Meanwhile, the rest of the team were continuing to run the general GHO clinic. This was only the second day of our clinics, and this was our last house for the day.

We walked up to the porch of a very small house, introduced ourselves and explained why we were in the country and visiting this area. We enjoyed talking with them with the help of our interpreter, and then we began sharing the gospel with three family members. Our in-country host mentioned that one of the family members had visited their church for the first time recently.

There were five GHO team members and one interpreter as well as a Nicaraguan church servant. Three of us shared parts of our testimonies and the gospel. As we continued to share, another three family members came to the windows and the doorway to listen. It was as though they were listening in the shadows. We could see the family members listening intently, and we just knew the Holy Spirit was working on their hearts and they were receiving the words of the gospel. When we gave them the opportunity to accept Christ, they said, "You need to talk to our father; we will not answer without his permission." So, we asked, "Where is your father? We would love to talk to him." This porch had a small section that wrapped around the side of the house, and they pointed in that direction.

Our culture is very individualistic, and if we accept Christ as our Savior, it has no significant effect on our family. Most other cultures are very relational, or community based, and a decision such as this would affect the entire family. We went in the direction they pointed, and there sat the father who appeared to be 70 years old or more. He had been listening to us the whole time, but just out of our sight. So, we approached him and asked permission for his family to respond to the opportunity of accepting Christ. He immediately gave us a "No."

We began to engage him in a conversation about the gospel, and he would not take his eyes off us as we spoke. However, he still would not allow his family to respond to the gospel, nor would he. At this point, we were way past our time for lunch, yet after talking to the interpreter, she felt the same as we did, that we could not leave. The Holy Spirit was keeping us there!

One of our team members used the clothesline that stretched the length of the porch as a tool to share the gospel. He explained that his pastor back home often uses a rope just like this one to share the gospel. He began by asking him to imagine the length of the rope goes on forever, and that this rope represents our eternal life. He then pointed to a piece of the rope the size of a finger and explained this small section of rope represents your life here on earth. Further, he explained that what you do with your small piece of rope here on earth determines where you will spend eternity.

The interpreter, Cari, then asked if she could speak to him one-on-one, in their native language, to be sure he understood everything that had been told to him. After about three minutes, we could see tears come to his eyes, his head began nodding up and down, and Cari started to smile. The father at that moment accepted Christ as his Lord and Savior and gave his family members the permission to answer the question of accepting Christ.

At this point, six family members were on the porch. We asked each family member individually if they wanted to accept Christ as their Lord and Savior. To our surprise, after the third or fourth family member accepted Christ, we heard a voice from in the house yell in English, "I am in!" The seventh family member was just inside the house listening the whole time. She also joined her family on the porch. All family members accepted Christ that day. There was a special joy and filling of the Spirit on that porch.

The next day we had our mid-week church service at the local church we were serving with and the whole family came to the service together! On our last day, as we were leaving the village, our bus drove by the house. As we went by, we slowed down and saw the whole family on the porch waving to us as we passed. It still brings me joy to remember that day and how faithful our God is and what a joy it is to be used as a vessel and messenger of the truth of the gospel. He is faithful to use the ones who say, "Here am I, Lord, send me," to glorify Him and His kingdom.

## This Jesus
### *Chuck Wood, DDS*

It's Wednesday of our clinic week, and I've just finished with a dental procedure on a young woman from an area just outside of Rio Grande, Nicaragua. She walked for an incredibly long time to receive dental treatment and, unknown to her, she also has a scheduled divine appointment with our Lord Jesus Christ.

After the dental treatment, I asked her through Juan, the interpreter, "Do you go to church?" She told me she lives very far away and there are no churches anywhere near her. I asked if she knew God.

"Oh yes, I know there is a God," she replied.

"What do you know about Jesus?" I asked.

"I have heard that he is his son but not much else."

I said, "Have you been saved? Have you accepted Jesus as your Savior?"

"No, what does this mean?" she replied.

With all of my patients on these mission trips I usually start my conversation with "Do you attend church" or "What would you like me to pray for you?" This conversation moves into a discussion about what is keeping them from having a relationship with the Lord. God generally brings to mind, after praying in my spirit, a Scripture lesson that I can use to disarm a person's excuse about making a connection with Jesus and coming to the saving grace of salvation. Praise God, I have had the honor of seeing many accept Christ as their Savior! This morning is the first time I have come across a person who has no experience with a church and so little knowledge of the Scriptures.

Dear God, where do I begin? I want so much to share the love of my Savior Jesus the Christ with this woman, but where do I start? Sitting on a hard-portable dental chair in the heat of the day I began sharing about what Jesus means to me. As the tears began to flow down our faces, as they are right now as I write about this, it was as if Jesus had just shown Himself and was giving me the words to say about the grace of God to save us sinners. After our beautiful time together, this woman said she wanted to know this Jesus as Lord and Savior and accept Him into her heart. All praise be to God who is full of mercy and grace. I can't describe the joy I felt when she made her commitment to the Lord. I felt I could almost hear the angels rejoicing as another name was added to the Book of Life.

It became important to me that this individual not be left alone as a new believer. But what to do as she lived so very far away from anyone who might be able to disciple her? It was extremely critical that she have a Bible. I went to see our team leader to find out if there were any Spanish Bibles available to give out. As there are just too many patients here in Rio Grande, it is impossible to have enough Bibles to go around. He did say he had just enough Bibles that were allotted as gifts for the local pastors, but he took a look in his box and found an extra Bible. "There isn't enough for everyone, but I'll leave it up to your good judgment whether this is where you should give this one Bible out." (I'm starting to cry again writing this, and I'm not usually this emotional. Honest.)

As I gave the Word of God to this new believer, you would have thought I was giving her something more precious than gold the way she held her new Bible. "I never dreamed I would possess a Bible! I have heard on the radio the person say turn to the book of... chapter... verse.... and I would say to my daughter, 'I wish I knew what this was.'"

"So, you have children?"

"Yes, I have three."

"It's important that you read this to them."

"Oh yes! I want to do this. I have an 11-year-old daughter who I want to read this also. Can I read this to my father?"

"Of course."

"I want my father to know this Jesus." (Here come those tears again).

I told her it was typical for a person to start at the beginning of a new book on page one and proceed to the end. I told her that this book is divided into two major parts, the Old Testament and the New Testament. She was informed that it was all good, but I suggested she begin with the New Testament. Start with the book of Juan. Our translator's name was Juan, and that would be easy to remember. As she would read the Word, there may be parts that might be difficult to understand, but don't be discouraged. It happens to all of us. Pray about it and just keep reading. God will be faithful to open the Scripture to her. As this new Christian would be homeschooling herself, she would definitely need our prayers. Juan told her that he and I would be praying for her. "You would pray for me? Then I will be praying for you." (There are those tears again; I can hardly see to write).

My story began with the "work of service" God had planned long before I had known I would be coming to Nicaragua. God had an appointment with this beautiful sister in Christ this Wednesday that has changed her destiny for eternity. She now will have an opportunity to make an impact with her children, her father and her community. She wasn't a Christian more than 15 minutes and the concept of making new disciples was already at work. Jesus told us to go to the ends of the earth and make disciples. For many of us, Rio Grande was pretty close to the end of the earth and outside our usual comfort zone. I shared this story with the head of GHO Nicaragua and he rejoiced with me over this new believer. He said, "You never know, she may open her home and start a new church in her home to share about 'this Jesus' in her area." This will be my prayer!

(It's okay, you can start tearing up with me now.)

# SIBERIA
## 61.0137° N, 99.1967° E

## I Will Build My Church
*Andy Sanders, MD*

As I write this, it is the best season of the year—college football season! Of course, I am always confident I am on the winning team, that in a few months I will have that great joy of seeing my team prevail against all others. Unfortunately, that confidence usually has disappeared by the third or fourth week. But what a neat feeling that victorious confidence is while it lasts.

Our healthcare mission teams go into dark corners throughout the world. There are a lot of forces against our teams that we face (government requirements, government agents, corruption, illnesses, unrest in the country and much more). And, then there are all the unseen, and far more powerful, forces that are against what we are doing. Ephesians 6:12 says it clearly: "For our struggle is not against flesh and blood, but against the rulers, against the powers, against the world forces of this darkness..." (NASB). Yet we are reassured in Matthew 16:19b, "I will build my church, and the gates of hell shall not prevail against it" (ESV).

It is a great feeling to know we are on the winning side. But on these teams, at times, the powers against us can seem quite strong and intimidating. Bit by bit, that victorious confidence can begin to disappear.

In Siberia, our healthcare mission team had an experience that helped to shed a light of reality on this. One day, our national partner took us into the forest outside of their town. We hiked into the woods, eventually ending at a little clearing. At the center of this clearing were a few strewn flowers and a slight indent in the ground. The story of this ground was then shared with us. In the early 1930s, Stalin's forces marched into town and arrested all the men in the church that they could find. These men were then dragged into the woods, forced to dig their grave and were killed as they stood in the pit, now just a slight indentation in the ground.

At the time of this martyrdom, it clearly looked like the real kingdom, the powerful kingdom, the victorious kingdom, was Stalin's kingdom. Prayers must have risen from the grave before the shots were fired for God's kingdom to come. Then, 80 years later our mission team was there. Stalin's kingdom has long since disappeared. There is a kingdom advancing there now, and it is the kingdom of God moving across that land.

We may be fooled at times, but it is all deception. There is one kingdom that will be victorious; "For the earth will be filled with the knowledge of the glory of the Lord as the waters cover the sea" (Habakkuk 2:14, NIV).

The kingdoms of the world cannot stop its advance. We are indeed on the winning team and victory is certain. That does not mean that hardships will not come, and battles might not ensue, but we can begin our mission trip with confidence, journey through our mission trip with confidence and end our mission trip confidently, knowing without a doubt that we are on the winning team. Our kingdom will advance. All other kingdoms will end. What a joy and privilege that we get to serve on such a team!

## My Thoughts Are Not Your Thoughts
*Andy Sanders, MD*

The mission team has a team leader. And the team leader has GHO leadership. A number of people are involved in "directing" this team, from its very beginning in preparing to go, to the travel there, throughout the time in the country and then back home again. How thankful we are for the leaders who, well, lead the team and the mission trip. As I stop now and think back on my teams, and on the leading of the mission work, a few memories jump right into the foreground of my thinking. One memory takes me back to Siberia and the other one to Nepal. Let me start in Siberia.

A ministry partner and I traveled there, seeking a possible door the Lord might open for us to bring a healthcare mission team there. We started by hosting a conference for some Siberian pastors. We met in a hotel deep in the woods somewhere. Our prayer was the Lord would show us if there was one Siberian pastor He might have for us to serve with. The Lord did give to us a certain pastor who shared our vision and heart. We soon found ourselves a few train rides deeper in Siberia visiting his city and church. During that visit, we traveled a few hours by car out to an area of multiple villages where a few thousand people around Russia and Europe had moved to follow some self-proclaimed messiah. While visiting that cult, we were invited into a cabin. In that cabin was a young mother and her sister who were both eager to hear about Christ. We had a translator, and she did a wonderful job for us as we shared the Good News. Before we left, they wished to accept Christ, and there in the cabin, in the middle of a cult, the two sisters turned from their sin and from the false savior to their true Savior and Lord.

Driving away, something was extremely clear to me. We had planned for a long time to bring a medical team to Siberia. We met pastors, we prayed for a Siberian partner, we traveled on many trains and hours in cars and ended up in that cabin. We had planned and planned our steps. "The mind of a person plans his way, But the Lord directs his steps" (Proverbs 16:9, NASB). It was He who knew of this village. It was He who knew of these two seeking hearts in that lone cabin. He had prepared two hearts to hear and to respond to the gift of redemption, and He used the planning of a healthcare mission trip to bring these two daughters into His family.

In Nepal, similarly, in a little fishing village that was a drive, a boat ride and a long hike from our hotel each morning, we had a little extra time one day at lunch. A few of us wandered out from the clinic to see if the Lord might allow us to share the gospel. I felt we should go to the left, but the others said right, and we turned right. I thought we should go to a certain house, but the others said to keep walking. "I will instruct you and teach you in the way which you should go; I will advise you with My eye upon you" (Psalm 32:8, NASB). Bit by bit we worked our way down the streets until a certain family called out for us to come to their home. By the end of that visit a 100-year-old man, 100 years in a Nepalese fishing village, 100 years of never hearing about Christ, turned to Christ, accepting Him as his Savior and Lord.

These two examples are multiplied countless times over on these healthcare teams. There is a leader, there is GHO leadership, but it is clear throughout each mission trip that the Leader is one who knows hearts and who knows where these seeking people are to be found. He leads the team, and He leads each individual on the team, throughout the trip, into the places and into the lives He has prepared from them. "'For My thoughts are not your thoughts, Nor are your ways My ways,' declares the Lord" (Isaiah 55:8, NASB).

A healthcare mission trip led by GHO is a wonderful thing to be a part of, but it is knowing that the team was led by the Lord, that you yourself were led by the Lord, that sets these teams infinitely apart from mere humanitarian medical teams. With our healthcare mission teams, we plan from the largest to the smallest details, but as we plan and go, we know it is the Lord Himself who will be directing the team and directing the steps of the team members into the lives He has prepared.

# UGANDA
## 1.3733° N, 32.2903° E

## Prayer Warriors
### *Sue Daily, Non-medical Servant*

Arriving with no luggage always makes a trip an adventure. We did not arrive at our overnight destination until 3 a.m. It was raining and the vehicle had broken down, so we walked to our room. Three days in the same clothes with only three hours of sleep is how I started a four-hour drive to our destination. We arrived around midnight and checked into a room. I had a bed with mosquito netting, a dirty sheet, a dirty pillow, a used damp towel, old red flip flops and a bucket of water. I poured the bucket of water over my head, dried off with the dirty damp towel and laid down under the netting. I watched the Geckos run up and down the wall and periodically turned my headlamp on to stop the hissing of the cockroaches. Sleep this night did not come easy. When morning came, I rolled out of bed thinking, "Is it worth it?"

During breakfast at a small third world dive restaurant, the waitress put a stack of bread from the neighboring table onto our table. She sat a bowl of cinnamon sugar down also. I took a piece of bread and sprinkled the sugar mixture on it. Much to my surprise, I was about to experience a whole new low as my cinnamon was moving. It was ants. Ugh!! Again, I was thinking, "Is it worth it?"

Arriving at the run-down brick church we found the children all waiting for us. Their teacher radiated with the glory of God. We ran our Bible camp, sang, played games and got to know the children. The afternoon brought time to share the gospel one on one. I shared with several. It was through heartfelt tears that three children accepted Christ. How awesome is this?

Is it worth? It is so worth it!! Shame on me for questioning God's plan. I tell this story so you will know how desperately we need our prayer warriors. I believe Satan puts doubts in our minds to hinder our dedication and service. I am grateful for those who hold me and our mission team up faithfully in prayer while we are on the mission field.

"...God of all comfort, who comforts us...that we may be able to comfort those who are in any affliction" (2 Corinthians 1:3-4, ESV).

# ZAMBIA
### 13.1339° S, 27.8493° E

## Before You Were Born, I Consecrated You
*Caroline Adams, RN*

When I was young, I would always ask God, "What happened? Why did my mother give me away? Why didn't my family want me? What was wrong with me and my sisters?" Now, I thank Him that He chose me to carry out His work. And He did it brilliantly.

I was born in Harlem, New York in 1953. Georgia, my mother, was part of the Great Black migration that brought many African Americans from the south to the north in the 1950s. They migrated to escape the horrors of Jim Crow laws that were so repressive to African Americans. When Georgia came to New York City, she was only 18, uneducated and unskilled. She could not find work and became involved with people who introduced her to men and alcohol. Between 1949 and 1953, Georgia gave birth to four beautiful daughters, but she was unable to take care of them because of poor choices and illness. Tuberculosis was rampant in New York City, and African American people were disproportionately affected by it. When she was pregnant with me (the youngest), she contracted tuberculosis and became very ill. I had to stay in the hospital for five weeks because of my exposure. Shortly after my birth, my sisters and I were placed in an orphanage and Georgia went to a sanitarium.

Georgia came from a large family in Moncks Corner, South Carolina. She had three brothers and four to five sisters. This family, unfortunately, is plagued by alcoholism and poverty, but they are very loving and loyal to one another. However, they did not want anything to do with my sisters and me. For many years I had so much resentment toward them, but the Lord forgives, and I must also.

God is so awesome! After two years in the orphanage, a pastor and his beautiful wife were led by the Lord to care for foster children, and they ended up becoming our parents. They adopted all four of us! I truly love the Lord because He gave us the best parents who ensured we were raised in the nurture and admonition of the Lord. Our parents were older but believed in giving us a beautiful childhood and a love for the things of the Lord. They also made sure we were educated; therefore, all of my sisters have a master's degree and one a PhD.

I can never forget how my life started off and how Jesus has led me all the way. The Lord told Jeremiah, "Before I formed you in the womb I knew you, And before you were born I consecrated you; I have appointed you a prophet to the nations" (Jeremiah 1:5, NASB). I am so blessed by His word. It is still true today. I may not be a prophet, but I have traveled all over with missions and have been a disciple to the nations.

In 2002, I had the pleasure of volunteering in an orphanage in Puebla, Mexico and knew the Lord had brought me full circle. There were the beautiful orphans with all the potential given to them by God. Recently, I traveled with GHO to care for orphans in Zambia. I was born to go! I saw myself and my sisters in every little girl coming off the bus. Their eyes were large with wonder and anticipation as we weighed and measured them. They were so polite and humble, but I also saw a strength of spirit. Dear Lord, please bless and protect these precious children. I cried, yes! I shed many tears because I know my Lord was taking care of these children through GHO just as He has always taken care of me.

During our week of clinic, we held a lady's tea event one evening for the women of the Zambian church we were serving alongside and with the ladies on our team. We spent time in praise and worship. We danced and raised our arms in praise to the beat of their beautiful music. I, along with a few other women on our team, was asked to share my testimony. The team leader had already talked about how, although they saw us as so different from them, we were all very much alike as well. We all had the same hopes and dreams, worries over our children and cares for our family. I was able to share about how I had been an orphan, yet graciously adopted into a God-fearing family. But at my heart, what I really wanted them to know was that every orphan we were caring for each day was a person. Not just another orphan, but a person. A future teacher. A future nurse or doctor. A person with his or her own hopes and dreams. I asked them to consider this as they did what they could to care for and minister to the thousands of orphans in Zambia.

After we had shared the team leader asked if any of the Zambian women would be willing to share. We heard from four, who poured out their testimonies of hurt and abuse, unanswered prayers and those He had answered, and how the Lord had protected them. We really are very much the same. We all have a journey to walk through with the Lord. Almost none of them are easy, particularly for those who begin as orphans. I believe this also blessed them as they were able to open up and share! They let us know that they had never gathered together as the women of the church before. We all learned a lot that day! They learned that they could live their lives together and help each other through, even if it is only as each other's prayer warriors. It was a beautiful, precious time with the Lord.

There is still so much work to be done. May the Lord continue to touch hearts. "...From everyone who has been given much, much will be demanded; and to whom they entrusted much, of him they will ask all the more" (Luke 12:48, NASB). I consider myself blessed to serve the Lord as long as I am able.

# GHO GENEALOGY

## GHO Beginnings
*David Stevens, MD, MA (Ethics)*
*CEO Emeritus, CMDA*

Global Health Outreach (GHO) was an idea, but not really a reality, in 1997. Medical Group Missions, CMDA's large short-term mission program, had decided to separate from CMDA in 1995 during my first year as CEO of CMDA. It was a traumatic parting, to say the least. That same year, the board had allowed me to sell our headquarters in Dallas, Texas and move the organization to Tennessee, an advantageous move for our fledgling ministry. Not one staff member who had worked at CMDA before I arrived came with us. So, we started over.

In the midst of the turmoil of all this, we "established" Global Health Outreach, but initially we partnered with other mission organizations and "co-branded" with their short-term teams. I then asked a physician friend to come lead GHO, but he barely lasted a year before he resigned. Things were not going well.

I then got a call from Prison Fellowship International, which initiated, trained and supported indigenous prison ministries in other countries. They asked me if we could send a short-term team to Zambia and, if that went well, perhaps other countries. Governments were putting pressure on them to "do something practical" for the prisoners if they were going to continue to have access for spiritual ministry, their primary focus. I knew this was an important opportunity for the kingdom and for GHO. Though I was extremely busy, I decided I would lead the first trip and began to recruit.

GOD SIGHTINGS

A prison is not an attractive mission site, and many of our "regular" participants were serving with our departed outreach. It was an uphill climb, and our departure date was looming. Then God intervened! Two phone calls not only birthed GHO but initiated a renaissance in healthcare missions.

None of the prisons in Zambia had dental services, but I had no dentists on the team. I knew a lot of physicians from my days leading Samaritan's Purse, but the only dentists I knew well were the two on the CMDA board. So, one day I picked up the phone and called one of them, Dr. Sam Molind. Without hesitation he said he would clear his schedule, recruit other dentists and serve as the team's dental director. Not only did he come, but he also paid the way for his dental assistant to come with him.

A few days later I got a call from David, a cardiologist and CMDA member, who said he would like to go on the trip and asked if he could bring some of the leaders in the mission program from his church. They had a good number of doctors, nurses and other healthcare personnel in the church. He explained they wanted to learn how to organize and lead their own medical teams. I said, "Sure!" We needed non-professional volunteers as well.

The prisons in Zambia were horrible. One prison that was designed for 500 prisoners back in colonial days had more than 2,000 inmates. They were locked in long warehouse-like buildings at night and had to sit with their legs around the prisoner in front of them to sleep. No medical care was provided at all. If you got seriously sick, you just died. Boys were in the same prisons as men. Unless you had money to hire a lawyer and bribe a judge, your case may never be heard. I remember a young boy of 12 who had been in prison for three years without trial for stealing a pair of tennis shoes. My heart broke to hear his story.

It was blistering hot, and we saw thousands of patients in dusty prison yards across the country. Half the team got food poisoning, including me. This physical "thorn "added to the dry, dusty misery we were seeing in our patients' faces. But those aren't the memories most deeply engraved in my mind. God did great things! Prisoners were hungry for hope and came in droves to kneel and accept Christ as one of our team members preached each late afternoon as we closed the clinic. I asked different team members to speak, and the day Sam spoke, I was startled when he gave his invitation. In the midst of all the dark-skinned bodies that had come forward to pray was a petite white girl kneeling with tears pouring down her face. It was Sam's dental assistant, who I learned later he had been witnessing to and praying for her to come to Christ for several years. She met Jesus in a filthy prison yard in Zambia!

One evening, exhausted and eager to find my bed, I was having supper with David and his church mission leaders to get to know them better and do some training. I asked about their church and their mission program. Making small talk turned into a big thing as they told their story. I was amazed to find their church had more than 20,000 people in attendance. They were already doing a health-focused missions conference for the hundreds of physicians, nurses, dentists and other healthcare personnel attending their church. Then God put an idea in my head. There was nothing to touch people's lives at the national level for healthcare missionaries or those considering that calling. What if this conference at Southeast Christian Church in Louisville, Kentucky could become the meeting, recruiting, networking and education place of healthcare missions? This was my greatest passion!

I broached the topic and we brainstormed ideas. We decided we needed to provide free housing in the homes of church members to get students and residents there. I could contact Nurses Christian Fellowship, Christian Pharmacy Fellowship and other Christian professional groups and ask them to co-sponsor the conference. I felt every group should "own it" as their conference, and then they would enthusiastically promote it to their members. We needed to keep the cost low for students and residents. We should invite mission organizations to exhibit. Ideas flowed like rushing water!

Soon after we returned to the U.S. from the trip, a group of leaders from the church traveled to Tennessee for a day of planning to continue to flesh out these ideas. I contacted many organizations and they jumped on board. The Global Missions Health Conference (GMHC) became a national reality, and it has had the greatest single impact on healthcare missions of anything that has happened in my lifetime.

God wasn't done yet! I had been very impressed with Sam's leadership and passion for evangelism on our trip together. He was still one of my bosses as a CMDA trustee, but during that trip we became friends. After that trip, I was still struggling to find God's person to lead GHO. As I prayed, God birthed a crazy idea in my mind—I should ask Sam to do it. Sam had a successful maxillofacial surgery practice in Vermont and was chief of staff at his hospital. His wife Dorothy led a crisis pregnancy ministry. He was an examiner for his specialty board. Many of his children and grandchildren lived nearby. For these and several other reasons, I doubted he would do it, but God persisted in nudging me. Faith is acting like God is telling the truth, so I picked up the phone and gave Sam a call. We had a great conversation and Sam said he and Dorothy would pray, but frankly, I still didn't have much hope. A few days later, Sam called and told me that God had clearly called them to lead GHO! When Sam arrived, Global Health Outreach really started and then grew and grew and grew some more.

During a difficult time in CMDA's history, we were surprised by joy! Looking back, God's hand on GHO is so clear, and for decades now we have seen the fruit of what He has done in and through GHO and in the lives of suffering people around the world. To Him be all praise!

## The Lord Gives Wisdom and Understanding
*Sam Molind, DMD*
*Director Emeritus, Global Health Outreach*

It was one of those things you can never forget. It seems like yesterday, even though it was in the year 2000 when I was doing a site visit to open a new outreach for the ministry of Global Health Outreach (GHO) in Ghana. During our time together in Ghana, I was to participate in the dedication ceremony of a new medical clinic in the far northern region of the country where 99 percent of the tribal people had never heard the gospel. The medical clinic was unique, as it had a clinic facility and housing for a nurse, physician and evangelist. The area's tribal kings and chiefs were invited to attend the dedication, but one king would not allow his chiefs or tribal members to go to the dedication because they were ancestral worshipers and practiced witchcraft. He did not want them exposed to the Christians. This is, of course, much of the reason they were opening a clinic in this area. "The Lord is not slow about His promise, as some count slowness, but is patient toward you, not wishing for any to perish, but for all to come to repentance" (2 Peter 3:9, NASB).

That Saturday evening after the dedication ceremony around 11 p.m., I was sleeping in the hallway of the clinic to try and find a breath of fresh, cool air in the midst of a great thunder and lightning storm that knocked out our lights when the clinic nurse brought to me a crying child and her screaming mother. The child was about eight years old and had stepped on a scorpion nest, receiving eight to 10 scorpion stings on his foot. He was in great pain, and his foot was swollen. I was informed by the nurse that the child was taken to the tribal witch doctor, whose potions and incantations were unable to help him. I gave the child some acetaminophen and asked the nurse if we had any antivenom in the clinic, but, unfortunately, we did not. I elevated the child's foot and put an ice pack on the area and told the nurse to ask if we could have a minute of prayer for her son. His mother agreed. As I prayed for her son, I felt the Lord give me some wisdom and understanding as to what to do. I asked the nurse to get me some Tetanus prophylaxis as the boy had never received any immunizations. I proceeded to give him some Benadryl and steroids and injected the area of the bites with local anesthesia to help eliminate the pain and dilute the venom. Before I sent them on their way, I told them to contact us as soon as possible if the child was not considerably better by the next day, as I would be leaving in the afternoon.

While we were packing up to leave on Sunday morning, some chiefs representing regional tribes came to invite us to come and see their king whose son we had helped during the night. We went there and were pleased to be well received. He was so happy to see his son treated and no longer in pain that he had a tribal celebration to make me a chief and to give me one of his wives if I would stay and help his people. I thanked him humbly and explained that, as a follower of Jesus, I had only one wife for a lifetime, and she was at home. I reached into my wallet and showed him a picture of Dorothy. I told him I appreciated his kind thoughtfulness and consideration and there would always be doctors at the healthcare clinic to help all the area tribes and they would always give them excellent care. We hugged each other and separated as great friends. I left with an overwhelming and enriched understanding and appreciation for how much our precious Lord loves all the people of the world and wants to reach out and give them every opportunity to hear the gospel and accept the Lord Jesus as their personal Savior and Lord. Praise Jesus! Hallelujah!

## The Sweet Surrender of "Yes"
*Trish Burgess, MD*
*Director, Global Health Outreach*

It is interesting to stop and think about pivotal moments in your life, particularly your spiritual life. Like the moment you first believed! I was already in my early 30s before I truly, wholeheartedly believed. I remember thinking how unbelievable this all seemed, yet the gospel has such a way of touching your heart with its deep and abiding truth. I remember the Lord immediately placing it on my heart to serve Him. I just couldn't wait, yet I knew I had so much to learn first. So, He spoke to me and told me to serve His children. I needed to learn Scripture. I needed to learn how to pray "out loud!" And I had young children myself, so it fit.

My husband and I were called to serve together, and we began by starting an AWANA program at our church. Not knowing any better, the blind leading the blind so to speak, I looked up the phone number for the regional AWANA missionary and arranged for him to come speak at our church. My husband and I were trained as leaders. We reached out to two other churches in the area and asked them to join us, and they did! It was a bold move for a girl who was a baby Christian, but I had a faith just bursting to be expressed and a heart to serve. I began teaching kindergarten through second graders. I quickly realized how strategic this was since this teaches a lot about Scripture memorization, which I did along with the children. I also did in-depth Bible studies. Along with this I began serving on a local retreat that taught me how to prepare and teach lessons from the Bible, how to share my testimony and how to live out a real, authentic faith. During this I discovered that I was a disciple! Wait, what? I am a disciple? The very idea of this thrilled me!

These were small moments of taking baby steps outside my comfort zone. This is largely how my faith began to grow! I stretched it to its limits, and each time I extended just a bit outside "my zone," God was there to help. So, just as Scripture promises, when I was faithful with small things, I was offered bigger things. Sometimes, I didn't necessarily want them, but there they were, none the less. My first big step, ginormous actually, was flying by myself to another country to meet a team of people I did not know. It was a Global Health Outreach (GHO) trip, and I was to serve as a doctor. I had a lump in my throat as I left my children and my husband dropped me off at the airport. I pictured one of those Olympic long jumpers, arms and legs flailing as they sailed through the air stretching to reach as far as they could. That was this step for me. Yet, at the same time, I knew I had to go. The Lord was just relentless. Have you ever been there? There was no saying "no" to God.

It was a pivotal moment in my life, because I discovered "why" on that mission trip. Mark Twain has a saying, "The two most important days in your life are the day you are born and the day you find out why." God spoke to me so clearly on that mission trip. He said three simple words, "This is it." And I knew in that instant what He meant. I was born to do healthcare missions for the Lord. That simple and that profound. The words of the song "One Pure and Holy Passion" rang through my head throughout that mission trip.

> Give me one pure and holy passion.
> Give me one magnificent obsession.
> Give me one glorious ambition for my life.
> To know and follow hard after you.
>
> To know and follow hard after you.
> To grow as your disciple in the truth.
> This world is empty, pale and poor
> Compared to knowing you, my Lord.
> Lead me on and I will run after you.
> Lead me on and I will run after you.

I have been a wholehearted follower of Christ and have been running after Him ever since! It was my passion, and my heart longed to serve in this manner. I prayed about this and told God if GHO was my ministry, then it needed to by my family's ministry as well. So, He said, "Take them." The five of us, including myself, my engineer husband and our three children, went on a GHO mission trip the next summer, and they all had a wonderful experience. From then on, they were fully on board when I was preparing for my next mission trip.

Another step of faith was when I was asked to consider being a team leader. Who, me? Yet, as I prayed over this, I explored this possibility by going to a GHO team leader training. I went to three of them actually, before the opportunity arose for me to lead a team. It was to Kenya, and I had such a heart for that country that I did a little happy dance when they gave it to me. It was one of the most challenging mission trips I had done, but it also felt right. I was sure I was walking within God's will for my life. I really enjoyed it and found myself in my happy place and comfort zone as I led this team every year, went on other GHO mission trips and continued with my emergency medicine work, home and family life. I found myself with a sweet little comfort zone. I am pretty sure we should put a warning sign on that zone! It never seems to last long before God is leading you back outside that comfortable little spot.

One of the "giant leap for mankind" kind of steps was next when I was asked, years later, to consider myself for the position of Director of Global Health Outreach. I was seriously shocked! It was one of those moments when you think someone is waving at you, yet you look over your shoulder to make sure they are not actually waving to someone behind you. You know! We have all been there. I honestly thought, "Surely there is someone much more qualified for this position than me." I had met, been mentored by and was friends with the two previous directors, Drs. Sam Molind and Don Thompson. I had served with both of them on the mission field. They were spiritual giants. So, I did what every "good Christian" does and replied that I was humbled and honored to be considered and would certainly pray about it.

Honestly, I had no intention of replying further. I assumed I was one of several and others would be more qualified than me. I also felt that this would be impossible for me. It would involve moving from my home, family, friends and church family of 18 years. My husband was training for a high-level position that would have been the pinnacle of his career. No way! Not possible. Yet, if you have ever tried to resist God, you know where I'm coming from. He calmly and patiently listens to all your arguments and then simply asks again. I tried to put the entire issue out of my mind. I really liked my comfort zone! But the Lord would not stop bringing it to mind. He is relentless! Have I mentioned that? I could not stop thinking about the possibility and what an amazing opportunity it would be. How could I say no? Yet, I simply could not ask my husband Scott to give up his career for mine once again. Over the years of our marriage, he moved with me for medical school, moved where I happened to match in residency and, once again, moved based on my career and job offers. He had sacrificed a lot. So, we were both praying about it but with very little discussion. This decision was agonizing. It is one thing to sacrifice for the Lord, but to ask your family to sacrifice as well? Finally, about two weeks after I interviewed and was offered the position, Scott finally said to me, "You know, Trish, it's just a job. We would be moving for ministry." And just like that, the door swung open wide to my saying yes.

All those steps along my faith journey with the Lord, from baby steps, long jumps and giant leaps for mankind, the Lord has shown Himself faithful. One really does just need a heart to serve Him and a faith that can be as tiny as a mustard seed. God has shown Himself through His word and in my life as one who does not necessarily call the equipped but equips the called. I stepped into this role way more confident than I should have, because I have learned through that initial "yes" all those years ago to serving Him on a GHO mission trip and all the opportunities along the way, that He is always with me and for me. And that is enough.

For more information about serving on a mission trip with Global Health Outreach, visit *www.cmda.org/gho*.

We welcome all variety of healthcare professionals and non-medical servants to join our teams as we bring the hope and healing only found in Jesus Christ to the least, the lost and the last around the world. You will be blessed more than you bless!

"Go therefore
and make disciples of all the nations,
baptizing them in the name of the Father and of the Son
and of the Holy Spirit, teaching them to observe all that I have
commanded you; and lo, I am with you always,
even to the end of the age"
(Matthew 28:19-20, NKJV).

The Christian Medical & Dental Associations exists to educate, encourage and equip Christian healthcare professionals to glorify God. Founded in 1931, CMDA is the largest community of Christian healthcare professionals and students in the world whose purpose is to change hearts in healthcare. CMDA continues to minister on a majority of medical and dental school campuses, trains students and graduates in leadership skills for effective practice and ministry, provides regional and national conferences for fellowship and education and provides opportunities for short-term mission trips as well as international academic and clinical teaching opportunities. CMDA also serves as a voice of its members to the media, churches and government by speaking out on bioethical, health and human rights issues.

For more information and to become a member, visit *www.cmda.org.*